Microsoft® Exchange 2000 Server

Administrator's Pocket Consultant

William R.
Stanek

PUBLISHED BY
Microsoft Press
A Division of Microsoft Corporation
One Microsoft Way
Redmond, Washington 98052-6399

Library of Congress Cataloging-in-Publication Data
Stanek, William R.
    Microsoft Exchange 2000 Server Administrator's Pocket Consultant / William R. Stanek.
        p. cm.
    Includes index.
    ISBN 0-7356-0962-4
    1. Microsoft Exchange Server (Computer file)   2. Client/server computing.   I. Title.

    QA76.9.C55 S78   2000
    005.7'13769--dc21   00-035149

Printed and bound in the United States of America.

1   2   3   4 5 6 7 8 9   MLML   5   4   3   2   1   0

Distributed in Canada by Penguin Books Canada Limited.

A CIP catalogue record for this book is available from the British Library.

Microsoft Press books are available through booksellers and distributors worldwide. For further information about international editions, contact your local Microsoft Corporation office or contact Microsoft Press International directly at fax (425) 936-7329. Visit our Web site at mspress.microsoft.com. Send comments to *mspinput@microsoft.com*.

Macintosh is a registered trademark of Apple Computers, Inc. Intel is a registered trademark of Intel Corporation. Active Client, Active Directory, Hotmail, Microsoft, Microsoft Press, MS-DOS, PowerPoint, Win32, Windows, and Windows NT are either registered trademarks or trademarks of Microsoft Corporation in the United States and/or other countries.

Unless otherwise noted, the example companies, organizations, products, people, and events depicted herein are fictitious. No association with any real company, organization, product, person, or event is intended or should be inferred.

Acquisitions Editor: Juliana Aldous
Project Editor: Julie Miller

Contents at a Glance

Part IV
Microsoft Exchange 2000 Server and Group Administration

Table of Contents

Part II
Active Directory Services and Microsoft Exchange 2000 Server

Part III
Microsoft Exchange 2000 Server Data Store Administration

crosoft Exchange 2000 Server Maintenance, onitoring, and Queuing   331

Managing the Exchange Server Service in Outlook 2000

When configured for Corporate Or Workgroup use, Outlook 2000 uses the Microsoft Exchange Server service to send and receive mail. This service has many advanced configuration and management options, including those for

- E-mail delivery and processing
- Remote mail
- Scheduled connections
- Multiple mailboxes

Each of these options is examined in the sections that follow.

Managing Delivery and Processing E-Mail Messages

In a corporate or workgroup environment, you have strict control over how e-mail is delivered and processed. Exchange mail can be delivered to one of three locations:

- Server mailboxes
- Personal folders
- Offline folders

Exchange mail can be processed by any of the information services configured for use in Outlook 2000. These information services include

- Microsoft Exchange Transport
- Microsoft Exchange Remote Transport
- Internet E-Mail

Let's look at how you use each of these delivery and processing options.

Using Server Mailboxes

Server mailboxes are the default configuration option. With server mailboxes, all mail is stored on the server and you can only view or send mail when you're connected to Exchange. Server mailboxes are best suited for corporate users with dedicated connections and for users who can remotely access Exchange through a dial-up connection.

If you want mail to be delivered to a server mailbox, complete the following steps.

1. In Outlook 2000, from the Tools menu, choose Services, and then select the Delivery tab.
2. The Deliver New Mail To The Following Location selection list shows where mail is being delivered. Select the Mailbox option, as shown in Figure 2-6.

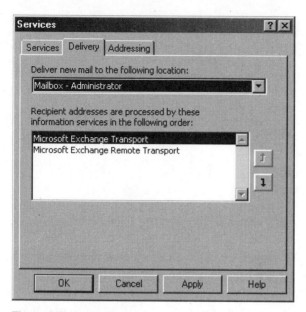

Figure 2-6. *In the Delivery tab, select the mailbox name rather than the names of personal or offline folders.*

Using Personal Folders

Personal folders are stored in a file on the user's computer. This file ends with the .pst extension. With personal folders, mail delivered to the user's Inbox is no longer stored on the server. One of the reasons users have personal folders is when Outlook 2000 is configured for Internet Only use. Users may also have personal folders if you specifically selected this option during setup or if the auto-archive feature is used to archive messages.

Real World Personal folders are best suited for mobile users who check mail through dial-up connections and who may not be able to use a dial-up connection to connect directly to Exchange. Users with personal folders lose the advantages that server-based folders offer—namely, single-instance storage and the ability to have a single point of recovery in case of failure. PST files have many disadvantages. PST files get corrupted frequently and on these occasions, the Inbox Repair Tool must be used to restore the file. If the hard drive on a user's computer fails, you can only recover the mail if the PST file has been backed up. Unfortunately, most workstations aren't backed up regularly (if at all) and the onus of backing up the PST file falls on the user who may or may not understand how to back up the PST file.

Determining the Availability of Personal Folders You can determine the availability of personal folders using either of these techniques:

- In the Outlook folder list, look for the Personal Folders node and related Deleted Items, Inbox, Outbox, and Sent Items folders.

- From the Tools menu, select the Services option, and then check the Services tab for the Personal Folders information service.

Creating Personal Folders If personal folders aren't available and you want to configure them, follow these steps.

1. In Outlook 2000, from the Tools menu, choose Services. On the Services tab, click the Add button.

2. In the Add Service To Profile dialog box, double-click Personal Folders. This displays the Create/Open Personal Folders File dialog box shown in Figure 2-7. Use this dialog box to look for an existing .pst file or to create a new one.

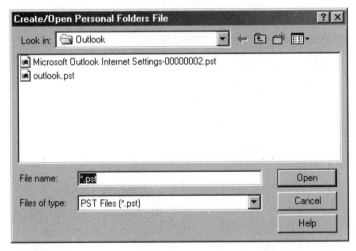

Figure 2-7. *Use the Create/Open Personal Folders File dialog box to search for an existing .pst file or create a new one.*

3. If you create a new .pst file, you'll see the Create Microsoft Personal Folders dialog box, and you'll need to configure a structure in which personal folders will be used. In the Outlook folder list, enter the name for the personal folders. Then, as necessary, select an encryption option and set a password on the .pst file. Click OK when finished.

Note It is important to be aware that Exchange Server does not ship with any password recovery utility for PST files. If a user sets a password on a PST file and forgets it, the Exchange administrator has no way to reset it. You may find third-party vendors who make password-cracking or recovery tools, but they are not guaranteed to work and they are not supported by Microsoft.

4. The personal folder you've selected or created is displayed in the Outlook folder list. You should see related Deleted Items, Inbox, Outbox, and Sent Items folders.

Delivering Mail to Personal Folders If you want mail to be delivered to a personal folder, complete the following steps.

1. In Outlook 2000, from the Tools menu, choose Services, and then select the Delivery tab.

2. Using the Deliver New Mail To The Following Location selection list, select the Personal Folders option, as shown in Figure 2-8.

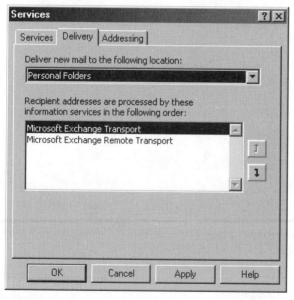

Figure 2-8. *To deliver mail directly to a personal folder and not store mail on the server, select the Personal Folders option from the Deliver New Mail To The Following Location selection list on the Delivery tab.*

Using Offline Folders

With offline folders, mail is stored on the server and copied to the offline folder file so that the user can view mail even when not connected to an Exchange server. Users have offline folders in only two situations: 1) offline folders were added manually or 2) during installation of Outlook 2000, the user answered Yes to the question "Do You Travel With This Computer?"

Tip You can think of offline folders as a mirror image of the folders stored in the user's mailbox on Exchange Server. Like personal folders, offline folders are stored in a file on the user's computer. This file ends with the .ost extension.

Creating Offline Folders Offline folders aren't available automatically, and you'll need to create them before you can use them. To create offline folders, follow these steps.

1. In Outlook 2000, select Tools, choose Synchronize, and then select Offline Folder Settings.

2. If offline folders haven't been configured previously, you'll see the prompt shown in Figure 2-9. This prompt tells you that you'll need to configure offline folders before you can create them. Click Yes.

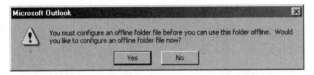

Figure 2-9. *A prompt will remind you that you must configure offline folder settings before you can create offline folders.*

3. Outlook displays the Offline Folder File Settings dialog box. The File field contains the default path for the offline folders. If you want to change this value, enter a new path or browse to a new folder location.

4. By default, offline folders use compressible encryption. This means that the folder file is encrypted in a format that can be compressed. For added security, select the Best Encryption option. Note, however, that with Best Encryption you won't be able to compress the file.

5. Click OK to create the offline folder file. If prompted to create the file, click Yes.

6. Once you create the offline folder file, you'll be able to select which folders you want to be available when working offline. As shown in Figure 2-10, you can select only folders in your server mailbox for offline use.

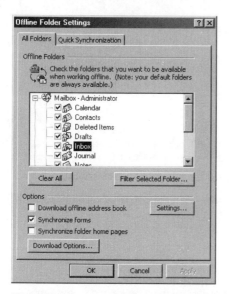

Figure 2-10. *In the Offline Folder Settings dialog box, select the folders you want to use and then configure options.*

7. After you select the folders to use offline, you can set individual filters on these folders. To create a filter, select a folder in the Folder view and then click the Filter Selected Folder button. Then create the filter for this folder.

 Note With filters, only messages matching all the specified criteria are downloaded for offline viewing. Other messages aren't downloaded.

8. Set additional options for offline viewing. These options include

- **Download Offline Address Book** Downloads the offline address book using the settings configured through the Offline Address Book dialog box.

- **Synchronize Forms** Synchronizes Exchange forms as well as folders.

- **Synchronize Folder Home Pages** Synchronizes folder home pages as well as the folders themselves.

- **Download Options** Sets specific download options that include message size limits and exceptions.

9. Click OK. Now you can synchronize the offline folders and the Exchange mailbox by selecting Tools, choosing Synchronize, and then choosing a synchronization option. To automatically synchronize based on certain events, follow the steps outlined in the section of this chapter entitled "Synchronizing Offline Folders."

Delivering Mail to Offline Folders   Offline folders are mirror images of server mailboxes. Their purpose is to allow you to view messages while you're offline without sacrificing all the benefits of storing mail on the server. If you want to view mail offline and bypass personal folders, complete the following steps.

1. In Outlook 2000, from the Tools menu, choose Services. This displays the Services dialog box.

2. The Microsoft Exchange Server service should be the first service listed and highlighted. Click the Properties button, or first click the Exchange Server service and then Properties.

3. Select the Advanced tab, and then select Enable Offline Use.

Note   The Enable Offline Use option is available only if you've previously created and configured offline folders.

Enabling and Disabling Offline Folders   If you've previously configured offline folders, you can enable or disable offline folders by completing the following steps.

1. In Outlook 2000, from the Tools menu, choose Options. This displays the Options dialog box. Select the Mail Services tab.

2. Enable offline folders by selecting Enable Offline Access.

3. Disable offline folders by clearing Enable Offline Access.

Changing Offline Folder Options   If you've previously configured offline folders, you can change offline folder settings by completing the following steps.

1. In Outlook 2000, from the Tools menu, choose Options. This displays the Options dialog box.

2. Select the Mail Services tab, and then make sure that Enable Offline Access is selected. Click Offline Folder Settings.

3. You can now change the offline folder settings, as described in Steps 6-9 of the section of this chapter entitled "Creating Offline Folders."

Synchronizing Offline Folders   Changes that users make to offline folders aren't automatically made in the associated server mailbox. Instead, the changes are updated only when the offline folders are synchronized with the server mailbox. For example, if Ted enters three new appointments in his calendar and the Calendar folder is configured for offline use, the changes aren't visible to other Exchange users. To make the changes visible, Ted will need to synchronize his offline folders with his server mailbox.

You can synchronize offline folders manually by doing either of the following:

• Press F9 to synchronize all folders.

• Select Tools, choose Synchronize, and then select a synchronization option.

You can configure automatic synchronization for offline folders by completing these steps.

1. In Outlook 2000, from the Tools menu, choose Options. This displays the Options dialog box.

2. Select the Mail Services tab, and then make sure that Enable Offline Access is selected. Use the following options to configure synchronization:

   • **When Online, Synchronize All Folders Upon Exiting**   Offline folders are synchronized when you exit and log off Outlook.

   • **When Online, Automatically Synchronize All Offline Folders** Offline folders are synchronized automatically according to the specified time interval, such as every 30 minutes.

   • **When Offline, Automatically Synchronize**   Synchronize all folders or only the mail and calendar folders using the specified time interval, such as every 30 minutes.

3. Click OK.

Using Remote Mail and Scheduled Connections

Remote mail and scheduled connections are two of the least understood configuration options for Exchange Server. Using these options, you can configure Outlook 2000 to connect to Exchange Server using a dial-up connection and then process mail using a very specific set of criteria. For example, you could have Outlook 2000 establish a dial-up connection to Exchange Server every 15 minutes, retrieving only messages with attachments that are sent directly to you. As you might imagine, setting such specific processing and retrieval options is fairly complicated, which is why most administrators configure remote Exchange connections using POP3 or IMAP.

When to Use Remote Mail and Scheduled Connections

Remote mail and scheduled connections are useful in these scenarios:

• Users at a branch office must connect to Exchange Server by means of dial-up connections.

• Laptop users want to connect to Exchange Server through dial-up connections when out of the office. (Here, you may want to configure on-site and off-site mail profiles for the user. See the section of this chapter entitled "Using Mail Profiles to Customize the Mail Environment.")

• Users working at home need to connect to Exchange Server by means of dial-up connections.

Configuring Remote Mail and Scheduled Connections

You configure remote mail and scheduled connections for Outlook 2000 by completing the following steps.

1. Start Outlook 2000, and then from the Tools menu, select Services. If you don't have the Services option (and have an Accounts option instead), the client

isn't configured for Corporate or Workgroup use and you must reconfigure mail support before continuing. For details, see the section of this chapter entitled "Reconfiguring Outlook 2000 Mail Support."

2. In the Services tab of the Services dialog box, double-click the entry for the Microsoft Exchange Server Profile. This displays the Microsoft Exchange Server dialog box.

3. With remote mail connections, you'll usually want to work offline and dial up as necessary. So select both Manually Control Connection State and Work Offline And Use Dial-Up Networking, as shown in Figure 2-11.

Figure 2-11. *Use the Microsoft Exchange Server dialog box to configure most Exchange Server service options, including remote mail, additional mailboxes, and offline folder settings.*

4. If you want to encrypt message traffic, click the Advanced tab and under Encrypt Information select the When Using Dial-Up Networking check box.

5. Select the Dial-Up Networking tab, and then choose an existing connection to use for remote mail, as shown in Figure 2-12. If no connection is available, click New and create a connection.

6. If you want the user to be prompted for connection settings, select Display Connection Dialogs At Logon. Otherwise, select Use The Following Settings At Logon and then type the necessary user name, password, and domain information.

Figure 2-12. *Outlook 2000 uses predefined dial-up connections to access Exchange Server. If no connections are listed in the Microsoft Exchange Server dialog box, click New to create one.*

7. You now need to configure remote mail. Select the Remote Mail tab, as shown in Figure 2-13.

8. If you'd like to remotely send and receive all mail with Exchange, select Process Marked Items and skip Steps 9-10.

9. If you'd like to receive only mail that meets specific criteria, select Retrieve Items That Meet The Following Conditions, and then click Filter. This displays the Filter dialog box shown in Figure 2-14. When using filters, keep in mind that only messages that match all the conditions specified are retrieved.

10. Use the options of the Filter dialog box to configure filters. These options are

   • **From** Enter names or e-mail addresses that must appear in the From field of messages. You can use semicolons (;) to separate multiple names or e-mail addresses.

   • **Sent Directly To Me** Transfers messages with the user's name in the To field.

Note When Send Directly To Me is selected, messages sent to distribution lists of which the user is a member aren't transferred . So be sure this is the behavior you want. If you want to transfer messages sent to distribution lists of which the user is a member, select Copied (Cc) To Me as well.

Figure 2-13. *In the Microsoft Exchange Server dialog box, you can check mail remotely and with scheduled connections.*

- **Copied (Cc) To Me**   Transfers messages with the user's name in the Cc field or messages sent to distribution lists of which the user is a member.

- **Subject**   Transfers messages with the specific subject. Multiple subjects can be entered as long as a semicolon separates each subject.

- **Advanced**   Allows you to specify additional criteria for messages to be transferred, including size, date, and importance.

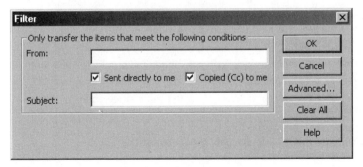

Figure 2-14. *The Filter dialog box lets you filter mail so it meets specified criteria.*

11. If you select Disconnect After Connection Is Finished in the Remote Mail tab, Outlook 2000 automatically disconnects after sending and receiving mail. This is optimum behavior when several people share a limited number of data lines.

12. If you'd like to send and retrieve mail at scheduled intervals, click Schedule, and then use these options of the Schedule Remote Mail Connection dialog box:

- **At Schedule**   A specific time to send and receive mail, such as 1 PM.

- **Every**   Set an interval in hours and minutes for sending and receiving mail, such as every 15 minutes or every hour.

13. As with remote mail, you can process all mail or set specific filter criteria.

14. Once you're finished configuring remote mail, click OK.

Accessing Multiple Exchange Server Mailboxes

Earlier in the chapter, I discussed how users could check multiple Internet mail accounts in Outlook 2000. You may have wondered if users could check multiple Exchange mailboxes as well—and they can. Users often need to access multiple Exchange mailboxes for many reasons:

- Help Desk administrators may need access to the Help Desk mailbox in addition to their own mailboxes.

- Managers may need temporary access to the mailbox of subordinates who are on vacation.

- Mailboxes may need to be set up for long-term projects, and project members will need access to those mailboxes.

- Resource mailboxes may need to be set up for accounts payable, human resources, corporate information, and so on.

Normally, there is a one-to-one relationship between user accounts and Exchange mailboxes. You create a user account and assign a mailbox to the account. Only this user can access the mailbox directly through Exchange. To change this behavior, you must do the following:

1. Log on to Exchange as the owner of the mailbox.
2. Delegate access to the mailbox to one or more additional users.
3. Have users with delegated access log on to Exchange and open the mailbox.

The sections that follow examine each of these steps in detail.

Logging On to Exchange as the Mailbox Owner

Logging on to Exchange as the mailbox owner allows you to delegate access to the mailbox. Before you can log on as the mailbox owner, you must complete the following steps.

1. Create a domain account for the mailbox, if one doesn't already exist.

2. Log on as the user. You'll need to know the account name and password for the domain.

3. Start Outlook 2000. Make sure that mail support is configured for Corporate or Workgroup use and that you can access Exchange Server. If necessary, configure support for Exchange Server, which creates the mail profile for the user.

4. Once you configure support for Exchange Server, you should be able to log on to Exchange Server as the mailbox owner.

Tip You should configure the mailbox to deliver mail to the server rather than to a personal folder. In this way, the mail is available to be checked by one or more mailbox users.

Delegating Mailbox Access

Once you've logged on as the mailbox owner, you can delegate access to the mailbox by completing these steps.

1. In Outlook 2000, from the Tools menu, choose Options. Select the Delegates tab, and then click Add.

2. In the Add Users dialog box, select the name of a user who needs access to the mailbox. As shown in Figure 2-15, click Add to put the name in the Add Users list. Repeat this step as necessary for other users. Click OK when you're finished.

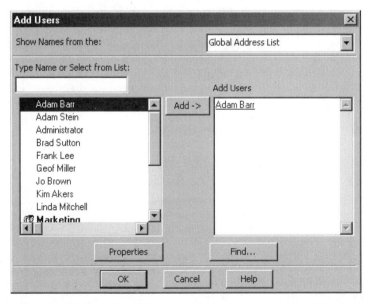

Figure 2-15. *Use the Add Users dialog box to assign delegate access to mailboxes.*

3. Click OK again. Delegated users can access the mailbox and send mail on behalf of the mailbox owner. To change this behavior, set folder permissions as described in the section of this chapter entitled "Granting Permission to Access Folders Without Delegating Access."

4. In the Delegate Permissions dialog box, assign permissions to the delegates for Calendar, Tasks, Inbox, Contacts, Notes, and Journal items. The available permissions are

- **None**   No permissions
- **Reviewer**   Grants read permission only
- **Author**   Grants read and create permissions
- **Editor**   Grants read, create, and modify permissions

 Note   If the user needs total control over the mailbox, you should grant the user Editor permission for all items.

5. Set any additional options, and then click OK. These changes are enforced when a user restarts Outlook.

Opening Additional Exchange Mailboxes

The final step is to let Exchange Server know about the additional mailboxes the user wants to open. To do this, follow these steps.

1. Have the user who wants access to additional mailboxes log on and start Outlook 2000.

2. In Outlook 2000, from the Tools menu, choose Services. In the Services dialog box, double-click the Microsoft Exchange Server information service entry.

3. Select the Advanced tab, and then click Add. Afterward, type the name of a mailbox to open. Generally, this is the same as the mail alias for the user or account associated with the mailbox. Click OK, and then repeat this step to add other mailboxes.

4. The additional mailboxes are displayed in the Outlook folder list.

Granting Permission to Access Folders Without Delegating Access

When a mailbox is stored on the server, you can grant access to individual folders in the mailbox. Granting access allows users to add the mailbox to their mail profiles and work with the folder. Users can only perform tasks for which you've granted permission.

To grant access to folders individually, follow these steps.

1. Right-click the folder for which you want to grant access, and then select Properties.

2. Select the Permissions tab, as shown in Figure 2-16.

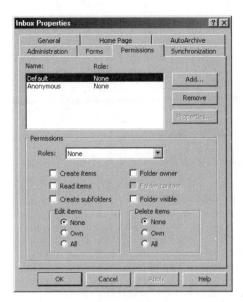

Figure 2-16. *Grant access to a folder through the Permissions tab.*

3. The Name and Role lists display account names and their permissions on the folder. Two special names may be listed:

   - **Default**   Provides default permissions for all users.

   - **Anonymous**   Provides permissions for anonymous users, such as those who anonymously access a published public folder through the Web.

4. If you want to grant users permission that's different from the default permission, click Add.

5. In the Add Users dialog box, select the name of a user who needs access to the mailbox. Then click Add to put the name in the Add Users list. Repeat this step as necessary for other users. Click OK when you're finished.

6. In the Name and Role lists, select one or more users whose permissions you want to modify. Afterward, use the Roles selection list to assign permissions or select individual permission items. The roles are defined as follows:

   - **Owner**   Grants all permissions in the folder. Users with this role can create, read, modify, and delete all items in the folder. They can create subfolders and can change permission on folders as well.

   - **Publishing Editor**   Grants permission to create, read, modify, and delete all items in the folder. Users with this role can create subfolders as well.

- **Editor**   Grants permission to create, read, modify, and delete all items in the folder.
- **Publishing Author**   Grants permission to create and read items in the folder, to modify and delete items the user created, and to create subfolders.
- **Author**   Grants permission to create and read items in the folder as well as to modify and delete items the user created.
- **Nonediting Author**   Grants permission to create and read items in the folder.
- **Reviewer**   Grants read-only permission.
- **Contributor**   Grants permission to create items but not to view the contents of the folder.
- **None**   Grants no permission in the folder.

7. When you're finished granting permissions, click OK.

Using Mail Profiles to Customize the Mail Environment

The mail profile used with Outlook 2000 determines which information services are available and how those information services are configured. A default mail profile is created when you install and configure Outlook 2000 for the first time. This mail profile is usually called MSExchange Settings.

The active mail profile defines the service setup for the user who is logged on to the computer. You can define additional profiles for the user as well. You can use these additional profiles to customize the user's mail environment for different situations. Here are two scenarios:

- A manager needs to check Technical Support and Customer Support mailboxes only on Mondays when she writes summary reports. On other days the manager doesn't want to see these mailboxes. To solve this problem, you create two mail profiles: Support and Standard. The Support profile displays the manager's mailbox as well as the Technical Support and Customer Support mailboxes. The Standard profile displays only the manager's mailbox. The manager can then switch between these mail profiles as necessary.

- A laptop user wants to check Exchange mail directly while connected to the local area network. When at home, the user wants to use remote mail with scheduled connections. On business trips, the user wants to use SMTP and POP3. To solve this problem, you create three mail profiles: On-Site, Off-Site, and Home. The On-Site profile uses the Exchange Server service with a standard configuration. The Off-Site profile configures Exchange Server for remote mail and scheduled connections. The Home profile doesn't use the Exchange information service and uses the Internet Mail service instead.

Common tasks you'll use to manage mail profiles are examined in the sections that follow.

Creating, Copying, and Removing Mail Profiles

You manage mail profiles through the Mail utility. To access this utility and manage profiles, follow these steps.

1. Click Start, choose Settings, and then select Control Panel.
2. In Control Panel, double-click Mail. This displays the settings for the active mail profile, which you can edit if necessary.
3. To display and manage other profiles, click Show Profiles. As Figure 2-17 shows, you should now see a list of mail profiles for the current user. Mail profiles for other users aren't displayed. You can now

   - Click Add to create a new mail profile using the Microsoft Outlook Setup Wizard.
   - Delete a profile by selecting it and clicking Remove.
   - Copy an existing profile by selecting it and clicking Copy.
   - View a profile by selecting it and clicking Properties.

Figure 2-17. *To add, remove, or edit mail profiles, click the Show Profiles button.*

Selecting a Specific Profile to Use on Startup

You can configure Outlook to use a specific profile on startup or to prompt for a profile to use. To start with a specific profile, follow these steps.

1. In Outlook 2000, from the Tools menu, choose Options, and then select the Mail Services tab.
2. After selecting Always Use This Profile, use the selection list to choose the startup profile.
3. Click OK.

To prompt for a profile before starting Outlook, follow these steps.

1. In Outlook 2000, from the Tools menu, choose Options, and then select the Mail Services tab.
2. Select Prompt For A Profile To Be Used.
3. Click OK.

The user will be prompted for a profile the next time Outlook is started.

Part II

Active Directory Services and Microsoft Exchange 2000 Server

Part II of this book will show you how to manage resources that are stored in the Active Directory database. You'll also learn about the Microsoft Exchange features that are integrated with Active Directory services. Chapter 3 examines essential concepts and tasks that you need to know to work with Exchange Server. Chapter 4 examines creating and managing users, mailboxes, and contacts. You'll learn all about Exchange aliases, delivery restrictions, storage limits, mailbox data stores, and more. In Chapter 5 you'll find a detailed discussion of how to use address lists, distribution groups, and templates. You'll also learn how to manage these resources. The final chapter in this part covers directory security and policies.

You can change the offline address list server by completing these steps:

1. Start System Manager, and then in the left pane (the Console Tree), click the plus sign (+) next to the Recipients node. Next, click the plus sign (+) next to the Offline Address Lists node.

2. Right click the offline address list that you want to modify, and then choose Properties.

3. The current offline address book server is listed in the Offline Address List Server field. To use a different server, click Browse, and then in the Select Exchange Server dialog box, choose a different server.

Customizing Address Templates

Have users ever asked you if you could change the fields in the Address Book for users, groups, or contacts? Chances are they have, and you probably said you couldn't. Well, you *can* customize the graphical interface for address book recipients, and the way you do it is to modify Exchange Server's address templates.

Using Address Templates

Address templates specify how recipient information appears in the Address Book. This graphical interface is unique for each type of recipient, including users, contacts, groups, and public folders. There are also templates for the address book search dialog box and the mailbox agent.

Each template has a predefined set of controls that describe its interface. These controls are

- **Label** Creates a text label in the template
- **Edit** Creates single-line text fields or multiline text boxes
- **Page Break** Specifies where a tab begins and where to set the text for the tab
- **Group Box** Creates a panel that groups together a set of controls
- **Check Box** Adds a check box with a text label
- **List Box** Adds a list box with optional scroll bars
- **Multi-Valued List Box** Adds a list box that can accept and display multiple values
- **Multi-Valued Drop-Down** Adds a selection list with multiple values

Each control has a specific horizontal (X) position and a specific vertical (Y) position in a dialog box. The control also has a specific width and height. The X, Y, width, and height values are set in screen pixels.

By modifying the controls within a template, you can change the way information is presented in the Address Book view. To learn how you can modify templates, see Figures 5-4 and 5-5. Figure 5-4 shows the default address book view for users. Figure 5-5 shows a modified address book view for users that is streamlined and simplified.

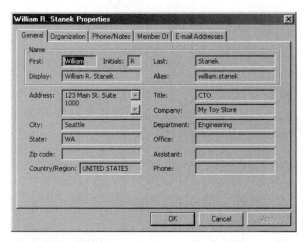

Figure 5-4. *The original Address Book view for users.*

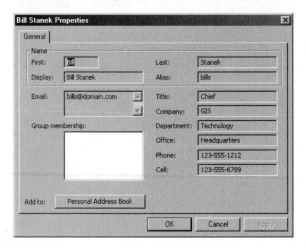

Figure 5-5. *A modified Address Book that combines fields from multiple tabs to create a view with a single tab.*

Modifying Address Book Templates

Modifying address book templates creates a custom view of the template that is available to all users in the organization. As you create the view, you'll have the opportunity to preview it so that you can check for mistakes. If you make a mistake, don't worry. You can restore the original template at any time.

You modify address book templates by completing these steps:.

1. Start System Manager, and then in the left pane (the Console Tree), click the plus sign (+) next to the Recipients node. Next, click the plus sign (+) next to the Address Templates node, and then select the template language you want to work with. For example, if you want to modify English language templates, select English.

2. You should see the available templates in the right pane. Double-click the template you want to modify.

3. Click the Templates tab. System Manager will read all the values defined in the template and the Active Directory attributes that are available for the related object. When System Manager is finished reading attributes, you'll see the complete set of controls available for the template (see Figure 5-6).

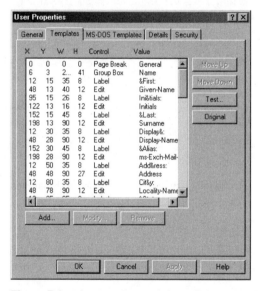

Figure 5-6. *The Templates tab lists all the controls that are assigned to the template.*

4. Click Test to preview the existing template. Study the template's configuration before you continue.

5. To add a new control to the template, click Add, and then choose a control type. Next, set the properties for the control, and then click OK. Click Test to check the modified view.

6. To update the settings of an existing control, select the control in the Templates tab, and then click Modify. After you modify the control's properties, click OK. Click Test to check the modified view.

7. To remove a control from the address book view, select the control in the Templates tab, and then click Remove.

8. Repeat Steps 5-7 until the template is customized to your liking. If necessary, use the Move Up and Move Down buttons to modify the position of controls in the scrolling list. If you need to restore the original view, click Original and then confirm the action when prompted.

9. When you're finished, close the Properties dialog box by clicking OK. Then rebuild the address lists as discussed in the section of this chapter entitled "Rebuilding Address List Membership and Configuration."

Restoring the Original Address Book Templates

When you modify address book templates, the original template files aren't overwritten and you can restore the original templates if you need to. Simply complete the following steps:

1. Start System Manager, and then in the left pane (the Console Tree), click the plus sign (+) next to the Recipients node. Next, click the plus sign (+) next to the Address Templates node, and then select the template language you want to work with.

2. You should see the available templates in the right pane. Double-click the template you want to restore.

3. Click the Templates tab. System Manager will go out and read all the values defined in the template and the Active Directory attributes that are available for the related object.

4. Restore the original view by clicking Original. When prompted, confirm the action by clicking Yes.

5. Close the Properties dialog box by clicking OK.

Repeat Steps 2-5 for other templates that you need to restore. Then rebuild the address lists in the manner described in the section of this chapter entitled "Rebuilding Address List Membership and Configuration."

Chapter 6

Implementing Directory Security and Microsoft Exchange 2000 Server Policies

In this chapter, you'll learn how to implement directory security and Microsoft Exchange 2000 Server policies. In Active Directory directory service, you manage security by using permissions. Users, contacts, and groups all have permissions assigned to them. These permissions control the resources that users, contacts, and groups have access to. They also control the actions that users, contacts, and groups can perform.

Exchange policies are useful administration tools as well. With policies, you can specify management rules for Exchange systems and Exchange recipients. *System policies* help you manage servers and information stores. *Recipient policies* help you manage e-mail addressing.

Controlling Exchange Server Administration and Usage

Users, contacts, and groups are represented in Active Directory as objects. These objects have many attributes that determine how the objects are used. The most important attributes are the permissions assigned to the object. Permissions grant or deny access to objects and resources. For example, you can grant a user the right to create public folders but deny that same user the right to view the status of the information store.

Permissions assigned to an object can be applied directly to the object, or they can be inherited from another object. Generally, objects inherit permissions from *parent objects*. A parent object is an object that is above an object in the object hierarchy. In Exchange 2000 Server, permissions are inherited through the organizational hierarchy. The root of the hierarchy is the *Organization node*. All other nodes in the tree inherit the Exchange permissions of this node. For example, the permissions on an administrative group folder are inherited from the Organization node.

You can override inheritance. One way to do this is to assign permissions directly to the object. Another way is to specify that the object shouldn't inherit permissions.

Assigning Exchange Server Permissions to Users and Groups

Several security groups have access to and can work with Exchange Server. These groups are Domain Admins, Enterprise Admins, Exchange Domain Servers, Exchange Enterprise Servers, and Everyone.

Domain Admins

Domain Admins are the designated administrators of a domain. Members of this global group can manage user accounts, contacts, groups, mailboxes, and computers. They can also manage messaging features, delivery restrictions, and storage limits. Nevertheless, they are subject to some restrictions in Exchange Server, and they don't have full control over Exchange Server. If a user needs to be an administrator of a local domain and manage Exchange Server, all you need to do is make the user a member of the Domain Admins group. By default, this group is a member of the Administrators group on the Exchange server and its only member is the local user, Administrator.

Enterprise Admins

Enterprise Admins are the designated administrators of the enterprise. Members of this global group can manage objects in any domain in the domain tree or forest. They have full control over Exchange Server and aren't subject to any restrictions. This means that unlike Domain Admins, Enterprise Admins can delete child objects and entire trees in Exchange Server. If a user needs full access to the enterprise and to Exchange Server, make the user a member of the Enterprise Admins group. By default, this group is a member of the Administrators group and its only member is the local user, Administrator.

Exchange Domain Servers

The Exchange Domain Servers group also has a special purpose. Members of this group can manage mail interchange and queues. By default, all computers running Exchange 2000 Server are members of this group, and you shouldn't change this setup. This domain global group is in turn a member of the domain local group Exchange Enterprise Servers.

Exchange Enterprise Servers

Exchange Enterprise Servers is a domain local group that you can use to grant special permissions to all Exchange servers throughout the domain forest. By default, the group has Exchange Domain Servers as its only member.

Everyone

The final group that has Exchange permissions is Everyone. Everyone is a special group whose members are implicitly assigned. Its members include all interactive, network, dial-up, and authenticated users. By default, members of this group can create top-level public folders, sub-folders within public folders, and named properties in the information store.

Understanding Exchange Server Permissions

Active Directory objects are assigned a set of permissions. These permissions are standard Microsoft Windows 2000 permissions, object-specific permissions, and extended permissions.

Table 6-1 summarizes the most common object permissions. Keep in mind that some permissions are generalized. For example, with Read Property and Write Property, *Property* is a placeholder for the actual property name.

Table 6-1. Common Permissions for Active Directory Objects

Permission	Description
Full Control	Permits reading, writing, modifying, and deleting
List Contents	Permits viewing object contents
Read Property	Permits reading a particular property of an object
Write Property	Permits writing to a particular property of an object
Read All Properties	Permits reading all object properties
Write All Properties	Permits writing all object properties
Delete	Permits deletion of object
Delete Subtree	Permits deletion of object and child objects
Modify Owner	Permits modifying the ownership of the object
Validate Write To ...	Permits a particular type of validated write
Extended Write To ...	Permits a particular type of extended write
All Validated Writes	Permits all types of validated writes
All Extended Writes	Permits all extended writes
Create Object	Permits creation of a specific object type
Delete Object	Permits deletion of a specific object type
Create All Child Objects	Permits creation of all child objects
Delete All Child Objects	Permits deletion of all child objects
Change Password	Permits changing passwords for the object
Receive As	Permits receive as the object
Reset Password	Permits resetting passwords for the object
Send As	Permits send as the object
Add/Remove Self As Member	Permits adding and removing object as a member

Table 6-2 summarizes Exchange-specific permissions. You use these extended permissions to control Exchange administration and usage. If you want to learn more about other types of permissions, I recommend that you read Chapter 13 of *Microsoft Windows 2000 Administrator's Pocket Consultant* (Microsoft Press, 2000).

Table 6-2. Extended Permissions for Exchange Server

Permission	Description
Add PF To Admin Group	Permits adding a public folder to an administrative group.
Administer Information Store	Permits administration of the Information Store.
Create Named Properties In The Information Store	Permits creation of named properties in the Information Store.
Create Public Folder	Permits creation of a public folder under a top-level folder.
Create Top-Level Public Folder	Permits creation of a top-level public folder.
Full Store Access	Permits full access to the Information Store.
Mail-Enable Public Folder	Permits mail-enabling a public folder.
Modify Public Folder ACL	Permits modification of the access control list on a public folder.
Modify Public Folder Admin ACL	Permits modification of the admin access control list on a public folder.
Modify Public Folder Deleted Item Retention	Permits modification of the deleted item retention period.
Modify Public Folder Expiry	Permits modification of a public folder's expiration date.
Modify Public Folder Quotas	Permits modification of a quota on a public folder.
Modify Public Folder Replica List	Permits modification of the replication list for a public folder.
Open Mail Send Queue	Permits opening the Mail Send queue and message queuing. The Exchange Servers group must have this permission.
Remove PF From Admin Group	Permits removal of a public folder.
View Information Store Status	Permits viewing the status of the Information Store.

Viewing Exchange Server Permissions

You can view security permissions for Exchange Server by completing the following steps:

1. Start System Manager, and then right-click the root or leaf level node you want to work with. Permissions are inherited from the Organization node by default. You can change this behavior.

2. From the pop-up menu, select Properties, and then in the Properties dialog box, click the Security tab, as shown in Figure 6-1.

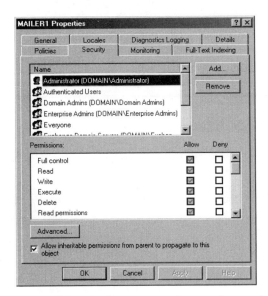

Figure 6-1. *Use the Security tab to configure object permissions.*

Note If the Properties option isn't available, you're trying to work with
a nonroot or nonleaf node, such as the Recipients, Administrative
Groups, or Servers nodes. Expand the node by clicking the plus sign (+),
and then select a lower-level node. Note also that for some nodes you
view and assign permissions through the Exchange Administration
Delegation Wizard. For details see the section of this chapter entitled
"Delegating Exchange Server Permissions."

3. In the Name list box, select the object whose permissions you want to view.
   The permissions for the object are then displayed in the Permissions list box.
   If the permissions are shaded, it means the permissions are inherited from a
   parent object.

Setting Exchange Server Permissions

You can control the administration and usage of Exchange Server in several ways:

- **Globally for an entire organization**   Set the permissions at the Organization level. Through inheritance, these permissions are then applied to all
  objects in the Exchange organization.

- **For each server**   Set the permissions individually for each server in the
  Exchange organization. Through inheritance, these permissions are then
  applied to all child nodes on the applicable server.

- **For each storage group** Set the permissions at the storage group level. Through inheritance, these permissions are then applied to all mailbox and public folder stores within the storage group.

- **For an individual node** Set the permissions on an individual node and disallow auditing inheritance for child nodes.

To set permissions for Exchange Server, follow these steps:

1. Start System Manager, and then right-click the root or leaf level node you want to work with.

2. From the pop-up menu, select Properties, and then click the Security tab in the Properties dialog box, as shown previously in Figure 6-1.

3. Users or groups that already have access to the Exchange node are listed in the Name list box. You can change permissions for these users and groups by selecting the user or group you want to change, and then using the Permissions list box to grant or deny access permissions.

 Note Inherited permissions are shown in gray. Override inherited permissions by selecting the opposite permission.

4. To set access permissions for additional users, computers, or groups, click Add. This displays the Select Users, Computers, Or Groups dialog box, shown in Figure 6-2.

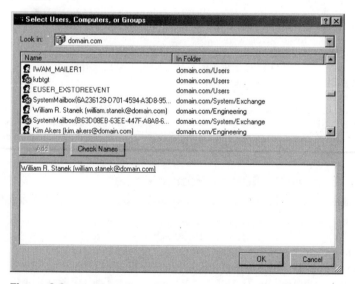

Figure 6-2. *Use the Select Users, Computers, Or Groups dialog box to select users, computers, or groups that should be granted or denied access.*

5. Use the Select Users, Computers, Or Groups dialog box to select the users, computers, or groups for which you want to set access permissions. You can use the fields of this dialog box as follows:

- **Look In** To access account names from other domains, click the Look In list box. You should now see a list that shows the current domain, trusted domains, and other resources that you can access. Select Entire Directory to view all the account names in the folder.
- **Name** The Name column shows the available accounts of the currently selected domain or resource.
- **Add** Add selected names to the selection list.
- **Check Names** Validate the user and group names entered into the selection list. This is useful if you type names in manually and want to make sure they're available.

6. In the Name list box, select the user, computer, or group you want to configure, and then use the fields in the Permissions area to allow or deny permissions. Repeat for other users, computers, or groups.

7. Click OK when you're finished.

Overriding and Restoring Object Inheritance

To override or stop inheriting permissions from a parent object, follow these steps:

1. Start System Manager, and then right-click the root or leaf level node you want to work with.

2. From the pop-up menu, select Properties, and then click the Security tab in the Properties dialog box.

3. Select or clear Allow Inheritable Permissions From Parent To Propagate To This Object.

Delegating Exchange Server Permissions

At times, you may need to delegate control of Exchange Server without making a user a member of the Domain Admins or Enterprise Admins groups. For example, you may want a technical manager to be able to manage Exchange mailboxes, or you may want your boss to be able to view Exchange settings but not be able to modify settings. The tool you use to delegate control of Exchange Server is the Exchange Administration Delegation Wizard.

Working With the Exchange Administration Delegation Wizard

You use the Exchange Administration Delegation Wizard to delegate administrative permissions at the organization level or the administrative group level. The level of permissions you set is determined by where you start the wizard. If you start the wizard from the organization level, the groups or users that you specify will have administrative permissions throughout the organization. If you start the wizard from the administrative group level, the groups or users that you specify will have administrative permissions for that specific administrative group.

To simplify administration, you should always assign permissions to a group, rather than assigning permissions to individual users. In this way, you grant permissions to additional users simply by making them members of the appropriate group, and you revoke permissions by removing the users from the group.

The Exchange Administration Delegation Wizard lets you assign any of the following administrative permissions to users and groups:

- **Exchange Full Administrator** Allows users or groups to fully administer Exchange system information and modify permissions. Grant this role to users who need to configure and control access to Exchange Server.

- **Exchange Administrator** Allows users or groups to fully administer Exchange system information but not to control access or modify permissions. Grant this role to users or groups who are responsible for the day-to-day administration of Exchange server.

- **Exchange View Only Administrator** Allows users or groups to view Exchange configuration information. Grant this role to users or groups that need to view Exchange configuration settings but are not authorized to make changes.

 Note The Exchange Administration Delegation Wizard controls access to Exchange 2000 Server. It doesn't give a user administrative access to the local machine. If Exchange administrators need to manage services or access the registry or file system on the server itself, you will need to make them local machine administrators for each Exchange Server they need to manage.

When setting permissions at the organization level, users and groups you delegate control to have the permissions shown in Table 6-3.

Table 6-3. Delegating Permissions at the Organization Level

Permission Type	Object	Permissions Granted	Do Permissions Apply to Subcontainers?
Full Administrator	Organization	All except Send As and Receive As permissions	Yes
Full Administrator	Exchange Container	Full Control	Yes
Administrator	Organization	All except Send As and Receive As permissions	Yes
Administrator	Exchange Container	All except Change permissions	Yes
View Only Administrator	Organization	View Information Store Status	Yes
View Only Administrator	Exchange Container	Read, List Object, List Contents	Yes

When setting permissions at the administrative group level, users and groups you delegate control to have the permissions shown in Table 6-4.

Table 6-4. Delegating Permissions at the Administrative Group Level

Permission Type	Object	Permissions Granted	Do Permissions Apply to Subcontainers?
Full Administrator	Organization	Read, List Object, List Contents	Yes
Full Administrator	Administrative group	All except Send As and Receive As	Yes
Full Administrator	Exchange container	Read, List Object, List Contents	No
Full Administrator	Connectors	All except Change permissions	Yes
Full Administrator	Offline Address Lists	Write	Yes
Administrator	Organization	Read, List Object, List Contents	Yes
Administrator	Administrative group	All permissions except Change, Send As, and Receive As	Yes
Administrator	Exchange container	Read, List Object, List Contents	No
Administrator	Offline Address Lists	Write	Yes
View Only Administrator	Organization	Read, List Object, List Contents	No
View Only Administrator	Administrative group	Read, List Object, List Contents, View Information Store Status	Yes
View Only Administrator	Exchange containers	Read, List Object, List Content	Yes (Limited)

Using the Exchange Administration Delegation Wizard

You use the Exchange Administration Delegation Wizard to set permissions by completing the following steps:

1. After starting System Manager, right-click the organization or administrative group for which you want to delegate administrative permissions, and then click Delegate Control. This starts the Exchange Administration Delegation Wizard.

2. Click Next.

3. In Users Or Groups, click Add to grant a new user or group administrative permissions. The Delegate Control dialog box is displayed.

4. Click Browse. Select the group or user to which you want to grant administrative permissions, and then click OK.

5. In the Delegate Control dialog box, use the Role selection menu to choose the administrative role. The options are

- Exchange Full Administrator
- Exchange Administrator
- Exchange View Only Administrator

6. Click OK. Repeat Steps 3-5 to delegate control to other users or groups.
7. Click Next, and then click Finish to complete the procedure.

Auditing Exchange Server Usage

Auditing lets you track what's happening with Exchange Server. You can use auditing to collect information related to information store usage, creation of public folders, and much more. Any time an action that you've configured for auditing occurs, this action is written to the system's security log, where it's stored for your review. You can access the security log from Event Viewer.

 Note To configure auditing, you'll need to be logged on using an account that's a member of the Administrators group, or be granted the Manage Auditing And Security Log right in Group Policy.

Setting Auditing Policies

To ensure the security and integrity of Exchange Server, you should set auditing policies. Auditing policies specify the actions that should be recorded in the security log. As with permissions, the auditing policies you apply are inherited by child objects in Exchange Server. Knowing this, you can configure auditing at several levels:

- **Globally** To apply auditing policies for all of Exchange Server, set the policies at the Organization level. Through object inheritance, these policies are then applied globally. But be careful; too many global policies can cause excessive logging, which will slow the performance of Exchange Server.

- **Per server** To apply auditing policies on a per server basis, set the policies individually on each server in the Exchange organization. Through inheritance, these policies are then applied to all sub-nodes on the applicable server. Again, you should try to limit the types of actions that you audit. If you don't, you may reduce the quality of performance of Exchange Server.

- **Per storage group** To apply auditing policies to a particular storage group, set the policies at the storage group level. Through inheritance, these policies are then applied to all mailbox and public folder stores within the storage group.

- **Per object** To apply auditing settings to a single node or object, set the policies on a specific node. Disallow auditing inheritance for child nodes as necessary.

Enabling Exchange Server Auditing

Before you can configure auditing for Exchange Server, you must enable the group policies for auditing. You can think of group policies as sets of rules that help you manage resources. You can apply group policies to domains, organizational units within domains, and individual systems. Policies that apply to individual systems are referred to as *local group policies* and are stored only on the local system. Other group policies are linked as objects in Active Directory.

You can enable Exchange auditing by completing the following steps:

1. Start Active Directory Users And Computers. In the console root, right-click the domain node, and then on the shortcut menu, select Properties.

Note The following steps explain how to enable auditing for an Active Directory domain. If you want a more detailed explanation of group policies and how they work, read Chapter 4 of *Microsoft Windows 2000 Administrator's Pocket Consultant (Microsoft, 2000).*

2. In the Properties dialog box, click the Group Policy tab. Edit the default policy by selecting Default Domain Policy, and then clicking Edit.

3. As shown in Figure 6-3, access the Auditing Policies node by working your way down through the console tree. Expand Computer Configuration, Windows Settings, Security Settings, and Local Policies. Then select Auditing Policies.

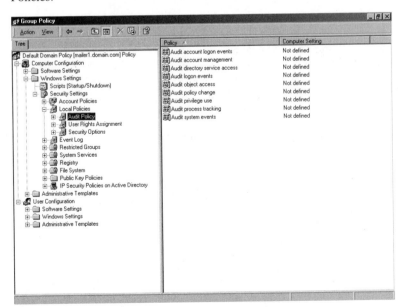

Figure 6-3. *Use the Audit Policy node in Group Policy to enable auditing.*

4. You should now see the following auditing options:

- **Audit Account Logon Events** Tracks events related to user logon and logoff.

- **Audit Account Management** Tracks account management by means of Active Directory Users And Computers. Events are generated any time user, computer, or group accounts are created, modified, or deleted.

- **Audit Directory Service Access** Tracks access to Active Directory. Events are generated any time users or computers access the directory.

- **Audit Logon Events** Tracks events related to user logon, user logoff, and remote connections to network systems.

- **Audit Object Access** Tracks system resource usage for mailboxes, information stores, and other types of objects.

- **Audit Policy Change** Tracks changes to user rights, auditing, and trust relationships.

- **Audit Privilege Use** Tracks the use of user rights and privileges, such as the right to create public folders.

- **Audit Process Tracking** Tracks system processes and the resources they use.

- **Audit System Events** Tracks system startup, shutdown, and restart, as well as actions that affect system security or the security log.

5. To configure an auditing policy, double-click its entry, or right-click the entry, and then select Security. This opens a Properties dialog box for the policy.

6. Select Define These Policy Settings, and then select either the Success or Failure check box, or both. Success logs successful events, such as successful logon attempts. Failure logs failed events, such as failed logon attempts.

7. Repeat Steps 5-6 to enable other auditing policies. The policy changes won't be applied until the next time you start the Exchange server.

Starting to Log Auditable Events

Once you've enabled auditing, you can start logging auditable events. To do this, complete the following steps:

1. In System Manager, right-click the node you want to work with, and then from the pop-up menu, select Properties. Click the Security tab, and then click Advanced.

2. In the Access Control Settings dialog box, click the Auditing tab. To inherit auditing settings from a parent object, make sure that Allow Inheritable Permissions From Parent To Propagate To This Object is selected.

3. Use the Auditing Entries list box to select the users, groups, or computers whose actions you want to audit. To remove an account, select the account in the Name list box, and then click Remove.

4. To add specific objects, click Add, and then use the Select User, Computer, Or Group dialog box to select an object name to add. When you click OK, you'll see the Auditing Entry For dialog box (see Figure 6-4).

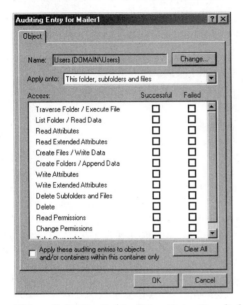

Figure 6-4. *Use the Auditing Entry For dialog box to set auditing entries for users, computers, and groups.*

5. Use the Apply Onto selection list to specify where objects are audited.

6. Select either the Successful or Failed check box, or both, for each of the events you want to audit. Successful logs successful events, such as successful file reads. Failed logs failed events, such as failed file deletions. The events you can audit are the same as those listed in Tables 6-1 and 6-2.

7. Click OK when you're finished. Repeat this process to audit other users, groups, or computers.

Exchange Server Recipient Policies

Auditing policies are only one type of policy that you can apply directly to Exchange Server. Another type of policy is a *recipient policy*. Recipient policies control e-mail address generation in the organization, and you also use them to establish new default e-mail addresses on a global basis.

Understanding Recipient Policies

You can apply recipient policies to all mail-enabled objects, including users, groups, and contacts. The first recipient policy created in the organization is set as the default.

The default policy establishes how default e-mail addresses are generated for cc:Mail, X.400, MS Mail, SMTP, and whatever other gateways may be installed in your Exchange organization. The default policy applies to all mail-enabled objects in the organization. By modifying the default policy, you can update the default e-mail addressing throughout the organization. Your updates can either override the existing e-mail addresses or be added as the primary addresses (with the current defaults set as secondary addresses).

You can create additional recipient policies as well. Through filters, you can apply these additional policies to specific types of objects and to objects matching specific filter parameters. Here are some examples:

- By filtering for specific objects, you could create different recipient policies for users, groups, and contacts. Here, you might have User, Group, and Contact policies.

- By filtering objects based on the department or division field, you could create recipient policies for each business unit in your organization. Here, you might have Marketing, Administration, and Business Development policies.

- By filtering objects based on the city and state, you could create recipient policies for each office in your organization. Here, you might have Seattle, New York, and San Francisco policies.

In an organization where many recipient policies are in effect, only one policy is applied to a particular object. To determine which of the policies is applied to an object, Exchange Server checks the policy's priority. Exchange Server applies a recipient policy with a higher priority before a recipient policy with a lower priority.

The default recipient policy is set to the lowest priority. This means that the default policy is applied only when no other policy is available for a particular object.

When you create a new recipient policy, the policy is applied based on the update interval of the Recipient Update Service running under the System Attendant. By default, the update interval is set to Always Run, which means that new policies are applied immediately. In a busy organization, however, continuous updating of e-mail addresses may degrade Exchange performance. That's why you can set the update interval to a different value. To determine or change the update interval, see the section of this chapter entitled "Scheduling Recipient Policy Updates."

Creating Recipient Policies

You use recipient policies to generate e-mail addresses for users, groups, contacts, and other mail-enabled objects in the organization. If your organization doesn't have a default recipient policy, the first policy you create is set as the default. You can't change some parameters of default policies. For example, you can't set filters on the default policy.

The default policy applies to all mail-enabled objects, and you can't change this behavior. Each additional policy that you create is fully customizable. You can set a name for the policy and add one or more filters.

You create a recipient policy by completing the following steps:

1. In System Manager, expand the Recipients node, and then select Recipient Policies. In the right pane, you should see a list of current policies.

2. Right-click Recipient Policies, point to New, and then click Recipient Policy.

3. In the Name field, type a name for the recipient policy. Use a descriptive name that makes it easy to determine how the policy is used and to which objects the policy applies.

4. Display the Find Exchange Recipient dialog box by clicking Modify. You can now select the recipient types that you want the new policy to apply to. Do this by selecting Show Only These Recipients, and then selecting the Users, Groups, and Contacts check boxes as appropriate.

5. As shown in Figure 6-5, use the options on the Advanced tab to set filters for the policy. These filters are based on object type. For example, if you wanted to filter users by division, you would click Field, point to User, and then select Division. Next, you would select a condition. The available conditions are Starts With, Ends With, Is (Exactly), Is Not, Present, and Not Present. You would then create the filter by clicking Add. To specify additional filters, you would repeat this process.

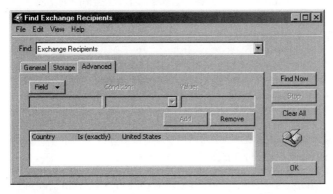

Figure 6-5. *Use the Advanced Options tab to set filters on individual objects.*

6. Click OK when you finish defining filters. The filter should now be displayed in the Filter Rules field of the General tab. If you made a mistake, you can edit the filter by clicking Modify again.

7. Click OK to create the policy. The policy is applied according to the schedule for the applicable Recipient Update service. To determine or change the update interval, see the section of this chapter entitled "Scheduling Recipient Policy Updates."

8. As necessary, modify the default e-mail addresses assigned, as described in "Modifying Recipient Policies and Generating New E-Mail Addresses."

Modifying Recipient Policies and Generating New E-Mail Addresses

Once you create recipient policies, they aren't etched in stone. You can change their properties at any time. The changes you make may cause Exchange Server to generate new e-mail addresses for recipients.

To modify a recipient policy, complete the following steps:

1. In System Manager, expand the Recipients node, and then select Recipient Policies.

2. In the right pane, you should see a list of current policies. Double-click the policy you want to modify.

3. If you want to rename the policy, type a new name for the policy in the Name field.

4. If you want to modify the way the policy is applied, click Modify, and then follow Steps 4-6 in the section of this chapter entitled "Creating Recipient Policies."

5. Click the E-Mail Addresses tab, as shown in Figure 6-6. You can now reconfigure the default e-mail address generation rules for the members of the recipient policy. Current rules are displayed in the Generation Rules field. You can now

   • **Create a new rule**   Click New. In the New E-Mail Address dialog box, select the type of e-mail address, and then click OK. Complete the Properties dialog box, and then click OK again.

   • **Change an existing rule**   Double-click the e-mail address entry, and then modify the settings in the Properties dialog box. Click OK.

   • **Delete a rule**   Select a rule, and then click Remove. Click Yes when prompted to confirm the deletion.

   • **Set a primary e-mail address**   When several e-mail addresses are defined for a particular gateway, you can specify a primary e-mail address. Simply select the address you want to be the primary one, and then click Set As Primary Address.

6. If you want the new e-mail addresses defined in the policy to become the primary addresses, and the current primary addresses to become alternative addresses, choose each new address in turn, and then select Set As Primary.

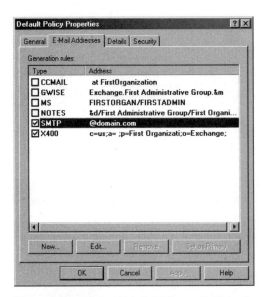

Figure 6-6. *Use the E-Mail Addresses Policy tab to specify how e-mail addresses should be generated.*

7. Click OK to apply the changes. If you modified the recipient membership or changed e-mail address settings, you'll see a prompt asking if you want to update all the corresponding recipient e-mail addresses. Click Yes to allow Exchange Server to generate new e-mail addresses based on the policy you've set.

Creating Exceptions to Recipient Policies

The Recipient Update Service is responsible for applying recipient policies. When you create new policies, the Recipient Update service running under the System Attendant applies these policies. A policy is applied only once—unless you modify a policy and cause Exchange Server to generate new e-mail addresses.

If you want to create exceptions to recipient policies, wait until the Recipient Update service has applied the policies. Then complete the following steps:

1. Start Active Directory Users And Computers, and then access the node that contains the recipients you want to work with.

2. Double-click the recipient object you want to exclude from the recipient policy, and then in the Properties dialog box, click the E-Mail Address tab. Now modify the e-mail address settings for the object that you selected:

   - **Add a new e-mail address** Click the New button. In the New E-Mail Address dialog box, select the type of e-mail address, and then click OK. Complete the Properties dialog box, and then click OK again.

- **Change an existing e-mail address** Double-click the address entry, and then modify the settings in the Properties dialog box. Click OK.

- **Delete an e-mail address** Select the address you want to delete, and then click Remove. Click Yes when prompted to confirm the deletion.

3. Click OK when you're finished, and then repeat this procedure for other recipients for whom you want to create policy exceptions.

Setting the Priority of Recipient Policies

As stated previously, only one recipient policy is applied to a recipient. This policy is the highest priority policy with filter conditions that match the properties of the recipient.

Priorities are assigned to recipient policies according to their position in the Recipient Policies list. In System Manager, you can view the current position and priority of a policy by expanding the Recipients node, and then selecting Recipient Policies.

The default recipient policy has the lowest priority, and you can't change this priority. You can, however, change the priority of other policies. You do this by right-clicking the policy in the Recipient Policies node, pointing to All Tasks, and then selecting Move Up or Move Down as appropriate. Changing the priority of policies may cause the Recipient Update Service to generate new e-mail addresses.

Scheduling Recipient Policy Updates

The Recipient Update Service is responsible for making updates to e-mail addresses, and it does this based on recipient policy changes. These updates are made at a specific interval that is defined for the service. You can view the update interval and modify it as necessary by completing the following steps:

1. Start System Manager, and then in the left pane (the Console Tree), click the plus sign (+) next to the Recipients node. Then select Recipient Update Services.

2. You should now see the available recipient update services in the right pane. You'll have an enterprise configuration service and one or more additional services for additional domains in the domain forest.

3. Right-click the service you want to work with, select Properties, and then use the Properties dialog box to view the service's configuration settings.

4. Use the Update Interval selection menu to choose a new update interval. The available options are

   - Always Run
   - Run Every Hour
   - Run Every 2 Hours

- Run Every 4 Hours
- Never Run
- Use Custom Schedule

Tip If you want to set a custom schedule, choose Use Custom Schedule, and then click Customize. You can now set times when the service should make updates using the Schedule dialog box shown in Figure 6-7. In this dialog box, you can set the detail of the view to be hourly or every 15 minutes. Each hour or 15-minute interval of the day or night is a field that you can turn on and off. Intervals where updates should occur are filled in with a dark bar—you can think of these intervals as being turned on. Intervals where updates shouldn't occur are blank—you can think of these intervals as being turned off. To change the setting for an interval, click it to toggle its mode (either on or off).

5. Click OK to apply the changes.

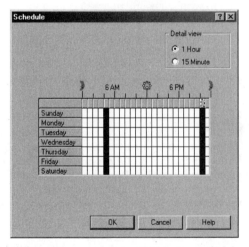

Figure 6-7. *In a busy Exchange organization, you may want to set a specific schedule for updates. If so, use the Schedule dialog box to define the update schedule.*

Forcing Recipient Policy Updates

Normally, the Recipient Update Service updates e-mail addresses at a specific interval. If necessary, you can manually start an update by completing the following steps:

1. Start System Manager and then, in the left pane (the Console Tree), click the plus sign (+) next to the Recipients node, and then select Recipient Update Services.

2. You should now see the available recipient update services in the right pane. You'll have an enterprise configuration service and one or more additional services for additional domains in the domain forest.

3. Right-click the service you want to work with, and then select Update Now.

Rebuilding the Default E-Mail Addresses

In some rare circumstances, the changes you've made to recipient policies may not be applied properly. If you think there's a problem, you may want to rebuild the default e-mail addresses for recipients. To do that, follow these steps:

1. Start System Manager and then, in the left pane (the Console Tree), click the plus sign (+) next to the Recipients node and then select Recipient Update Services.

2. You should now see the available recipient update services in the right pane. You will have an enterprise configuration service and one or more additional services for additional domains in the domain forest.

3. Right-click the service you want to work with, and then select Rebuild. When prompted to confirm the action, click Yes.

 Caution The process of rebuilding e-mail addresses can take several hours. If you cancel the process before it's completed by either stopping the service or rebooting the Exchange server, you'll need to rebuild the addresses again.

Deleting Recipient Policies

You can delete any recipient policies that you create by right-clicking the policy, selecting Delete, and then confirming the action when prompted. The Address List service will update the e-mail addresses for the affected recipients as necessary. If for some reason these updates don't occur, you can manually start an update as described in the section of this chapter entitled "Forcing Recipient Policy Updates."

 Note You can't delete the default recipient policy. This policy is mandatory.

Exchange Server System Policies

Exchange Server supports three types of system policies: server, mailbox store, and public folder store. These policies control settings for Exchange servers and information stores.

Using System Policies

You configure system policies through a set of property pages. With mailbox store policies, you can use the General, Database, and Limits property pages to configure a policy. With public store policies, you can use the General, Database, Replication, and Limits property pages to configure a policy. With server policies, you can use only the General property page to configure a policy.

The properties pages are used as follows:

- **General** Sets general-purpose options for the policy
- **Database** Sets storage group membership, Exchange database names, and maintenance schedules
- **Replication** Sets the replication interval and message size limits
- **Limits** Sets the deleted item retention interval and storage limits

When you create a policy, you don't have to use all of the available property pages. Instead, you select only the property pages you want to use. Later, if you want to add or remove property pages, you can do so by changing the property page availability. The property pages are displayed in the Properties dialog box for the policy as tabs.

You don't manage system policies in the same way that you manage recipient policies. Instead of creating a policy and relying on a service to implement it, you must take charge of each step of the creation and implementation process. For most system policies, the creation and implementation process works like this:

1. You create a server, mailbox store, or public store policy.
2. You specify the servers or stores to which the policy should apply by adding items to the policy.
3. You enforce the policy by applying it.

You can create multiple policies of a particular type, and you can apply all of these policies to the same objects. For example, you could create separate mailbox store policies to apply database, replication, and messaging controls. You could then apply these policies to the same mailbox store.

If two policies conflict, you'll be notified of the conflict when you create the policy, and you'll have the opportunity to remove the item from the conflicting policy. If you don't rectify the conflict, you won't be able to add the item to the policy. To see how this would work, consider the following scenario:

You create a policy that sets a storage limit on all mailbox stores in the Exchange organization, and then create a new policy that removes the storage limit on the Technology mailbox store. You're notified that a conflict exists and you're given the opportunity to remove the Technology mailbox store from the first policy.

As you work with these policies, you'll note that you could use other techniques to set some of the options. For example, you can set deleted item retention

- Through the properties of individual mailboxes
- Through the Mailbox Store Properties dialog box
- Through mailbox store policies

The differences among these techniques are ones of scope and manageability. With mailbox properties, you're setting per mailbox limits that affect a single mailbox. With mailbox store properties, you're setting limits on individual mailbox stores, which can affect multiple mailboxes. With mailbox store policies, you're setting limits on one or more mailbox stores and all of the related mailboxes.

Policy settings also take precedence, and in some cases they disallow configuring options at other levels. For example, if you set a deleted item retention period in a mailbox store policy, you can't edit the deleted item retention period in an affected mailbox store. You can override the policy settings only on individual mailboxes.

Creating Server Policies

Server policies set message tracking and logging rules for Exchange servers in an organization. Message tracking allows you to track messages sent within the organization, messages received from external mail servers, and messages coming from or going to foreign mail systems. With message tracking enabled, you can track system messages, e-mail messages, and public folder postings.

There are many reasons for using message tracking. You can use message tracking to

- Track a message's path from originator to recipient
- Search for messages sent by specific users
- Search for messages received by specific users
- Confirm receipt of messages
- Monitor the organization for inappropriate types of messages

To create a server policy, complete the following steps:

1. Start System Manager. Under the Administrative Group node, click the plus sign (+) next to the administrative group you want to edit. Right-click the System Policies node, and point to New. Then click Server Policy. If no System Policies node is listed, right-click the administrative group where you want to create the policy, point to New, and then select System Policy Container. The available options are General, Database, Limits, and Full-Text Indexing.

2. In the Policy Manager dialog box, select the General check box, and then click OK. You'll see a Properties dialog box.

3. Type a descriptive name for the policy.

4. As shown in Figure 6-8, you configure the server policy options using the General (Policy) tab. Policies you can set include

- **Enable Subject Logging And Display** Logs all subject fields for messages processed by the server.

- **Enable Message Tracking** Tracks all messages processed by Exchange Server.

- **Remove Log Files** Removes all log files older than the value set in Remove Files That Are Older Than (Days) field. The valid range is from 1 to 99 days.

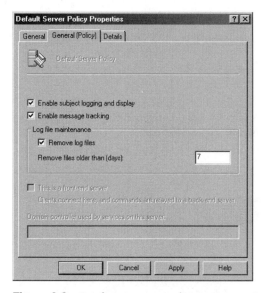

Figure 6-8. *Configure server policy options using the General (Policy) tab.*

5. Click OK to create the policy. Keep in mind that you can't modify settings that are inherited from server policies, and they appear disabled in the Server Properties dialog box.

6. Add items to the policy, and then apply the policy, as discussed in the sections of this chapter entitled "Adding Items to a System Policy" and "Applying a System Policy."

Creating Mailbox Store Policies

Mailbox store policies set storage limits, deleted item retention intervals, and maintenance rules for mailbox stores in the Exchange organization. You can't modify settings that are inherited from mailbox store policies, and they appear disabled in the Mailbox Store Properties dialog box.

You create a mailbox store policy by completing the following steps:

1. Start System Manager. Under the Administrative Group node, click the plus sign (+) next to the administrative group you want to edit. Right-click the System Policies node, point to New, and then click Mailbox Store Policy. If no System Policies node is listed, right-click the administrative group where you want to create the policy, point to New, and then select System Policy Container.

2. In the Policy Manager dialog box, select the property pages you want to use in the policy. The available options are General, Database, Limits, and Full-Text Indexing.

3. When you click OK, you'll see a Properties dialog box.

4. Type a descriptive name for the policy.

5. As shown in Figure 6-9, you use the General (Policy) tab to set default messaging options. The only mandatory setting is the default public store. All other settings are optional. The available options are

   - **Default Public Store**   Shows the default public store for the mailbox store. To set this value, click the corresponding Browse button, select a public store to use, and then click OK.

   - **Offline Address List**   Shows the default offline address list for the mailbox store. To set this value, click the corresponding Browse button, select an offline address list to use, and then click OK.

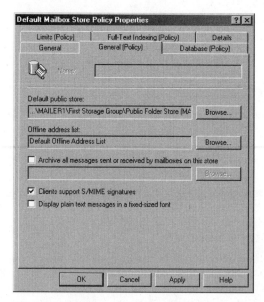

Figure 6-9. *For mailbox store policies, set general messaging options using the General (Policy) tab.*

Viewing and Understanding Logons

The information store tracks logons to mailbox and public folder stores. You can use this information to view a wide range of activity in the data store.

To view logon information, follow these steps:

1. In System Manager, select the Exchange 2000 server you want to manage and then click the plus sign (+) next to the storage group you want to work with.

2. You should see a list of available data stores. Click the plus sign (+) next to the data store you want to examine and then select Logons.

3. As Figure 8-8 shows, information about all logons to the store is displayed in the Details pane. The default view provides basic logon information, such as the user name, the related Windows 2000 account, the logon time, the last access time, and the client version.

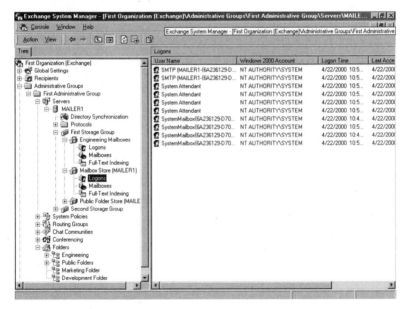

Figure 8-8. *The Logons node provides summary information for all logon activity in the data store.*

To get more detailed logon information, you can customize the logon view. Right-click Logons, point to View, and then click Choose Columns. Next, use the Modify Columns dialog box to add or remove columns from the view. Table 8-1 provides a summary of the available columns. Use the extra information provided to help you track logons and related data store activity.

Table 8-1. Understanding the Column Headings in the Logon Details

Column Name	Description
Client Version	The version of the client that was used to log on.
Code Page	The code page that the client was using, such as 1252.
Folder Ops	The total number of folder operations performed in the last 60 seconds. Operations tracked include opening, closing, and renaming folders.
Full Mailbox Directory Name	The full e-mail address of the mailbox being accessed. This option is available only for mailbox stores.
Full User Directory Name	The name of the mailbox that is accessing the mailbox store.
Host Address	The IP address of the client.
Last Access Time	The date and time the user last accessed the mailbox store.
Locale ID	The locale ID for the language the client is using.
Logon Time	The date and time that the user last logged on.
Messaging Ops	The total number of messaging operations performed in the last 60 seconds. Operations tracked include opening, closing, and deleting messages.
Open Attachments	The total number of open attachments.
Open Folders	The total number of open folders.
Open Messages	The total number of open messages.
Other Ops	The total number of miscellaneous operations performed in the last 60 seconds.
Progress Ops	The total number of progress operations performed in the last 60 seconds. Progress operations tell users how long it takes to complete a task.
Stream Ops	The total number of stream operations performed in the last 60 seconds. Operations tracked include changing and deleting attachments.
Table Ops	The total number of table operations performed in the last 60 seconds. Operations tracked include displaying folder contents and expanding public folder tree views.
Total Ops	The total number of operations performed in the last 60 seconds.
Transfer Ops	The total number of transfer operations performed in the last 60 seconds. Operations tracked include copying and moving messages.
User Name	The full name of the user who last logged on, such as William R. Stanek.
Windows 2000 Account	The Windows 2000 account name of the user who last logged on, such as DEV\williams.

Typically, you'll use custom views to help you understand the level of activity in a particular data store. Generally, you're most interested in seeing

- Who accessed the store
- Which IP addresses were used
- What was the last access time
- How many messages and attachments are open
- What was the total number of operations performed in the last 60 seconds.

A custom view to provide this information would include these columns:

- User Name
- Host Address
- Last Access Time
- Open Messages
- Open Attachments
- Open Folders
- Total Ops

Viewing and Understanding Mailbox Summaries

Just as you can view information about logons, you can also view information about mailboxes. The available information tells you

- How many messages are stored in a mailbox
- How much space the mailbox is using
- Whether the mailbox has deleted items that are being retained
- How long items have been deleted
- Whether the mailbox is subject to storage limits
- Who the last user to log on to the mailbox was

You can view mailbox summaries by completing the following steps:

1. In System Manager, select the Exchange 2000 server you want to manage and then click the plus sign (+) next to the storage group you want to work with.
2. You should see a list of available data stores. Click the plus sign (+) next to the mailbox store you want to examine and then select Mailboxes.
3. As Figure 8-9 shows, mailbox summaries should now be displayed in the Details pane. The default view provides basic mailbox information, such as the mailbox name, the last user account to log on to the mailbox, the mailbox size, and the total number of items in the mailbox.

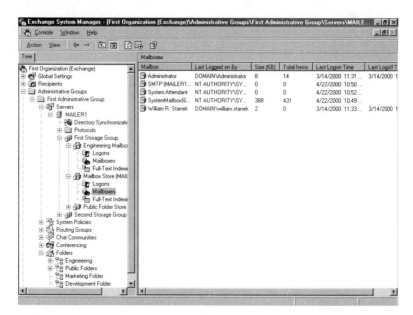

Figure 8-9. *The Mailboxes node provides information that can help you track mailbox usage.*

To get more detailed mailbox information, you can customize the mailbox view. Right-click Mailboxes, point to View, and then click Choose Columns. Next, use the Modify Columns dialog box to add or remove columns from the view. Table 8-2 provides a summary of the available columns. Use the extra information provided to help you track mailbox activity.

Table 8-2. Understanding the Column Headings in the Mailbox Details

Column Name	Description
Deleted Items (KB)	The total amount of disk space, in kilobytes, occupied by deleted items that are being retained for the mailbox.
Last Logged On By	The account name of the user who last logged on to the mailbox.
Last Logoff Time	The time that a user last logged off this mailbox.
Last Logon Time	The time that a user last logged on to this mailbox.
Mailbox	The mailbox name.
Size (KB)	The total amount of disk space, in kilobytes, that a mailbox occupies.
Storage Limits	Specifies whether a mailbox is subject to storage limits.

(continued)

Table 8-2. *(continued)*

Column Name	Description
Total Associated Messages	Total number of system messages, views, rules, and so on, associated with the mailbox.
Total Items	Total number of messages, files, and postings that are stored in the mailbox.
User Deleted Time	The date and time at which Exchange Server detected the deletion of the user account for this mailbox.

Mounting and Dismounting Data Stores

You can access only data stores that are mounted. If a store isn't mounted, the store isn't available for use. This means that an administrator has probably dismounted the store or that the drive on which the store is located isn't online.

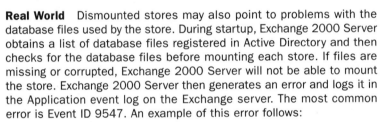

Real World Dismounted stores may also point to problems with the database files used by the store. During startup, Exchange 2000 Server obtains a list of database files registered in Active Directory and then checks for the database files before mounting each store. If files are missing or corrupted, Exchange 2000 Server will not be able to mount the store. Exchange 2000 Server then generates an error and logs it in the Application event log on the Exchange server. The most common error is Event ID 9547. An example of this error follows:

```
The Active Directory indicates that the database file
D:\Exchsrvr\mdbdata\Marketing.edb exists for the Microsoft
Exchange Database /o=My Organization/ou=First Administrative
Group/cn=Configuration/cn=Servers/cn=MAILER2/cn=Marketing,
however no such files exist on the disk.
```

This error tells you that the Exchange database (MARKETING.EDB) is registered in Active Directory but Exchange 2000 Server is unable to find the file on the disk. When Exchange 2000 Server attempts to start the corrupted mailbox store, you'll see an additional error as well. The most common error is Event ID 9519. An example of this error follows:

```
Error 0xfffffb4d starting database First Storage
Group\Marketing on the Microsoft Exchange Information Store.
```

This error tells you that Exchange 2000 Server couldn't start the Marketing database. To recover the mailbox store, you must restore the database files as discussed in Chapter 10 under "Recovering Exchange Server." If you are unable to restore the database files, you can recreate the store structures in System Manager by mounting the store. When you mount the store, Exchange 2000 Server creates new database files and as a result, all the data in the store is lost and cannot be recovered. Exchange 2000 Server displays a warning before mounting the store and recreating the database files. Only click Yes when you are absolutely certain that you cannot recover the database.

Checking the Mount Status of Data Stores

To determine whether a store is mounted, follow these steps:

1. In System Manager, select the Exchange 2000 server you want to manage and then click the plus sign (+) next to the storage group you want to work with.

2. You should see a list of available data stores in the Details pane. The icon to the right of the data store name indicates the mount status. If the icon shows a red down arrow, the store isn't mounted.

Dismounting Data Stores

You should rarely dismount an active data store, but if you need to, follow these steps:

1. In System Manager, select the Exchange 2000 server you want to manage and then click the plus sign (+) next to the storage group you want to work with.

2. You should see a list of available data stores in the Details pane. The icon to the right of the data store name indicates the mount status. If the icon shows a red down arrow, the store is already dismounted.

3. Right-click the store you want to dismount, select Dismount Store, and then confirm the action by clicking Yes. Exchange Server dismounts the store. Users accessing the store will no longer be able to work with their server-based folders.

Mounting Data Stores

If you've dismounted a data store to perform maintenance or recovery, you can remount the store by completing the following steps:

1. In System Manager, select the Exchange 2000 server you want to manage and then click the plus sign (+) next to the storage group you want to work with.

2. You should see a list of available data stores in the Details pane. The icon to the right of the data store name indicates the mount status.

3. You should see a red down arrow indicating that the store isn't mounted. If so, right-click the store and then select Mount Store.

4. If Exchange Server is able to mount the store, you'll see a dialog box confirming that the store has been mounted. Click OK.

5. The new store isn't accessible to users that are currently logged on to Exchange server. Users will need to exit and then restart Outlook before they can access the newly mounted store.

Specifying Whether a Store Should Be Automatically Mounted

Normally, Exchange Server automatically mounts stores on start up. You can, however, change this behavior. For example, if you're recovering Exchange server from a complete failure, you may not want to mount data stores until you've completed recovery. In this case you may disable automatic mounting of data stores.

To enable or disable automatic mounting of a data store, complete the following steps:

1. In System Manager, select the Exchange 2000 server you want to manage and then click the plus sign (+) next to the storage group you want to work with.

2. Right-click the data store you want to work with and then select Properties.

3. Select the Database tab in the Properties dialog box.

4. To ensure that a data store isn't mounted on start-up, select Do Not Mount This Store At Start-Up.

5. To mount the data store on start-up, clear Do Not Mount This Store At Start-Up.

6. Click OK.

Setting the Maintenance Interval

You should run maintenance routines against data stores on a daily basis. The maintenance routines organize the data store, clear out extra space, and perform other essential housekeeping tasks daily from 1:00 A.M. to 5:00 A.M. By default, Exchange Server runs maintenance tasks daily at 11:00 P.M. If this conflicts with other activities on the Exchange server, you can change the maintenance time. To do that, follow these steps:

1. In System Manager, select the Exchange 2000 server you want to manage and then click the plus sign (+) next to the storage group you want to work with.

2. Right-click the store you want to work with and then select Properties.

3. Select the Database tab in the Properties dialog box, and then use the Maintenance Interval selection menu to set a new maintenance time. Select a time (such as Run Daily From 11:00 P.M. to 3:00 A.M.) or Use Custom Schedule.

4. Click OK.

Tip   If you want to set a custom schedule, choose Use Custom Schedule and then click Customize. You can now set times when maintenance should occur.

Checking and Removing Applied Policies

You use mailbox and public folder policies to control settings for groups of data stores. When a policy applies to a property, the property is dimmed and you're unable to change its value in the data store's Properties dialog box. The only way you can change a policy-controlled property is to

- Edit the related policy
- Remove the policy from the data store

To determine whether a policy applies to a data store, follow these steps:

1. In System Manager, select the Exchange 2000 server you want to manage and then click the plus sign (+) next to the storage group you want to work with.

2. Right-click the store you want to work with and then select Properties.

3. Any policies that affect the data store are listed in the Policies tab. You can modify or delete the policy by following the techniques discussed in the sections of Chapter 6 entitled "Modifying System Policies" and "Deleting System Policies."

Renaming Data Stores

To rename a data store, follow these steps:

1. In System Manager, select the Exchange 2000 server you want to manage and then click the plus sign (+) next to the storage group you want to work with.

2. Right-click the data store, select Rename from the shortcut menu, and then type a new name for the storage group.

 Note All objects in Active Directory directory service are located by a unique identifier. This identifier uses the directory namespace and works through each element in the directory hierarchy to a particular object. When you change the name of a data store, you change the namespace for all the objects in the data store.

Deleting Data Stores

Deleting a data store removes the data store and all the public folders or mailboxes it contains. Before you delete a data store, make sure that you no longer need the items it contains. If they are needed, you should move them to a new data store. You move mailboxes as described in the section of Chapter 4 entitled "Moving a Mailbox to a New Server or Storage Group." You move public folders as described in the section of Chapter 9 entitled "Renaming, Copying, and Moving Public Folders."

Once you've moved items that you may need, you can delete the data store by completing the following steps:

1. In System Manager, select the Exchange 2000 server you want to manage and then click the plus sign (+) next to the storage group you want to work with.

2. Right-click the data store you want to delete and then select Delete from the shortcut menu.

3. When prompted, confirm the action by clicking Yes.

Chapter 9

Using and Replicating Public Folders

Public folders are one of the most underused and least understood aspects of Microsoft Exchange Server. Administrators often avoid using public folders because they think they're difficult to configure and impossible to manage. Nothing could be further from the truth. Public folders add great value to any Exchange organization, especially if users need to collaborate on projects or day-to-day tasks.

If you want to learn to use and replicate public folders, this chapter will show you how. Unleashing the power of public folders is what it's all about.

Making Sense of Public Folders and Public Folder Trees

Public folders are used to share files and messages within an organization. To maintain security, each public folder can have very specific usage rules. For example, you could create public folders called CompanyWide, Marketing, and Engineering. While the CompanyWide folder would be accessible to all users, the Marketing folder would be accessible only to users in the marketing department and the Engineering folder would be accessible only to users in the engineering department.

Public folders are stored in a hierarchical structure referred to as a *public folder tree*. There is a direct correspondence between public folder trees and public folder stores. You can't create a public folder store without first creating a public folder tree, and users can access public folder trees only when they're part of a public folder store. The only public folder tree accessible to Messaging Application Programming Interface (MAPI) clients, such as Microsoft Outlook 2000, is the default public folder tree. You can access other public folder trees in compliant Web browsers and Microsoft Windows applications. You can also access public folders through the Installable File System (IFS).

You can replicate public folders to multiple Exchange servers. These copies of folders, called *replicas*, provide redundancy in case of server failure and help to distribute the user load. All replicas of a public folder are equal. There is no master replica. This means that you can directly modify replicas of public folders. Folder changes are replicated automatically to other servers.

Public folder trees define the structure of an organization's public folders. Each tree has its own hierarchy, which you can make accessible to users based on criteria you set. While public folder trees are replicated to all Exchange servers in the organization, folder contents are replicated only to designated servers. These servers host replicas of public folder data. Two types of public folder trees are used with Exchange 2000 Server:

- **Default**   This tree, referred to as the MAPI Clients tree in System Manager, is the only tree accessible to MAPI clients. Each Exchange 2000 server in the organization has a default public folder store that points to this tree. In System Manager, the default name for this tree is Public Folders. In Outlook, you access this tree through the All Public Folders node.

- **Alternate**   Alternate trees provide additional public folder hierarchies for the Exchange organization but are accessible only to compliant Web browsers and Windows applications. In System Manager, alternate trees are referred to as General Purpose trees.

Web browsers and other applications can remotely access public folder trees using WebDAV (Web Distributed Authoring and Versioning). Another way to access a public folder is to use IFS. The next section of this chapter explains how to access public folders using WebDAV and IFS.

Accessing Public Folders

Unlike previous versions of Exchange Server, where access to public folders was limited, Exchange 2000 Server makes it possible to access public folders just about anywhere. You can

- Access public folders through e-mail clients
- Access public folders through network shares
- Access public folders on the Web or the corporate intranet

The following sections explain each of these techniques.

Accessing Public Folders in E-Mail Clients

You can access public folders from just about any e-mail client, provided the client is MAPI compliant. The recommended client is Outlook 2000. When Outlook 2000 is configured for corporate or workgroup use, users have direct access to the Public Folders tree but not to alternate trees. When Outlook 2000 is configured for Internet-only use, users can access public folders only when their client is configured for IMAP.

If Outlook is configured properly, users can access public folders by completing the following steps:

1. Start Outlook 2000. If the Folder List isn't displayed, click View, and then select Folder List.

2. In the Folder List, expand Public Folders to get a complete view of the available top-level folders. A top-level folder is simply a folder at the next level below the tree root.

Note Chapter 2 discusses techniques you can use to configure Outlook. Refer to the section of that chapter entitled "Configuring Mail Support for Outlook 2000 and Outlook Express."

Accessing Public Folders as Network Shares

Another way to access a public folder is to use IFS. IFS allows Windows applications to access public folders in much the same way as these applications access network shares.

IFS is installed automatically on the M drive of an Exchange 2000 server. Administrators can access public folders and other shared data sources on the M drive. The M drive has the following basic features:

- A domain folder for each available domain
- A mailbox (MBX) folder that is the root for all mailboxes on the Exchange server
- A Public Folders folder that is the root of the default public folder tree

These folders aren't shared by default. If users need to access public folders on the M drive, you can create a network share for the public folder. You should not, however, share the domain folder or the MBX folder without carefully considering the security risks.

Note Creating network shares is covered in detail in Chapter 13 of *Microsoft Windows 2000 Administrator's Pocket Consultant* (Microsoft Press, 2000). There you'll find complete instructions for creating shares and managing share permissions.

Accessing Public Folders from the Web

You use WebDAV to access public folders over the World Wide Web and the corporate intranet. WebDav is an extension to the Hypertext Transfer Protocol, HTTP. Using HTTP and WebDav, clients can create and manage public folders and the items they contain. One way to do this is to access a public folder through an HTTP virtual server hosted by Exchange 2000 Server. Simply type the folder's URL into the browser's Address or Location field.

To access the public folder tree in a browser, you type the URL ***http:// servername/public,*** where *servername* is a placeholder for the HTTP virtual server hosted by Exchange 2000 Server and public is the default name of the Public Folders Web share. You can access alternate public folder trees through their Web share as well.

Exchange 2000 Server automatically configures Web sharing, and you can check the sharing configuration by completing the following steps:

1. Exchange 2000 Server stores public folders and other shared data sources on the M drive. Use Windows Explorer to access this drive.

2. Right-click the public folder, and then from the pop-up menu, select Properties.

3. In the Properties dialog box, click the Web Sharing tab, which is shown in Figure 9-1.

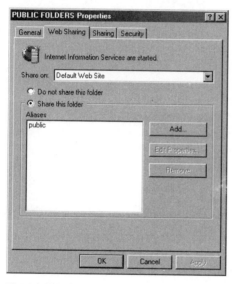

Figure 9-1. *Use the Web Sharing tab to check the configuration of the shared folder. If other administrators inadvertently changed settings, you should change the settings back to the defaults used by Exchange Server.*

4. The name for the folder's Web share is shown in the Aliases field. This is the name that users type into the browser's Address field after the server name. For example, if the alias was set to /GroupFolders, you could access the folder as **http://servername/GroupFolders/**. The Web share name is not case-sensitive.

5. Click the alias in the Aliases field, and then click Edit Properties. You can now check the access and application permissions for the share. By default, Exchange Server grants certain access permissions. To allow reading, writing, and directory browsing, you should make sure that these permissions are granted as well. The default permissions granted to the folder are

   - Read
   - Write

- Script Source Access
- Directory Browsing

6. Since all application permissions are denied, Application Permissions should be set to None.

Real World   Most problems with Web sharing of public folders can be traced to individuals who inadvertently change the default share settings. If you restore the original settings, users will regain access to the public folder. Keep in mind, however, that there may be reasons for not sharing a public folder over the Web—document security is one. Also note that only Exchange Server can initialize Web sharing for public folders. If Exchange Server isn't sharing public folders correctly, you may have incorrectly configured Internet Information Services or Outlook Web Access. See Chapter 13 for details on working with IIS and Outlook Web Access.

Creating and Managing Public Folder Trees

The sections that follow discuss key creation and management tasks for public folder trees. The only type of tree that you can create, change, or delete is an alternate tree. You can't create, change, or delete the default public folder tree. The default tree is created automatically when Exchange 2000 Server is installed and is managed by Exchange 2000 Server.

Creating Public Folder Trees

When you create a new public folder tree, Exchange Server creates an object in Active Directory directory service that represents the tree. The directory object holds the properties and attributes of the tree and must be stored in a specific container. A default container is automatically created in the Exchange organization. If you want to use a different container, you must create the container before you create the public folder tree.

You need to create additional containers for public folder trees only when you use administrative groups. With administrative groups, each group that you create after the first group can have a public folders container. To create this container, follow these steps:

1. Start System Manager. Click Start, point to Programs, point to Microsoft Exchange, and then click System Manager.

2. Expand Administrative Groups, and then expand the group you want to work with. If the group already has a Folders node, a public folder tree has already been created and you can't create another. If the group doesn't have a Folders node, right-click the group, point to New, and then choose Public Folders Container.

3. You can now create public folder trees in the container.

To create a public folder tree, follow these steps:

1. Start System Manager. Click Start, point to Programs, point to Microsoft Exchange, and then click System Manager.

2. If Administrative groups are displayed, expand Administrative Groups, and then expand the group you want to work with.

3. In the left pane (the console tree), right-click Folders, point to New, and then click Public Folder Tree.

4. Type a descriptive name for the public folder tree. To make the tree easier to access in Web browsers, don't use spaces in the tree name. Some browsers don't understand spaces, and users may have to type the escape code **%20** instead of a space.

5. Click OK. To make the new tree available for use, create a public folder store that uses the tree. See the section of Chapter 8 entitled "Creating Public Folder Stores."

Once you've created a public folder tree and added it to a public folder store, authorized users can create subfolders within the tree that can be used to meet different collaboration requirements. These additional folders can contain other folders, items, and messages.

Designating Users Who Can Make Changes to Public Folder Trees

By default, all users can create folders in the public folder tree. To change these security settings and allow only specific users or groups to make changes, you'll need to perform the following tasks:

1. Use the procedures outlined in the section of Chapter 6 entitled "Setting Exchange Server Permissions" to designate users and groups who can

   - Create public folders
   - Create top-level public folders
   - Create named properties in the Information Store

2. Remove security permissions for the group Everyone.

3. Confirm that the changes are appropriate by testing the security controls.

Renaming, Copying, and Moving Public Folder Trees

You can manipulate public folder trees in much the same way that you can manipulate other objects. To rename a public folder tree, follow these steps:

1. In System Manager, right-click the public folder tree you want to work with.

2. Select Rename, type a new name, and then press ENTER.

3. If the tree is associated with a public folder store, Exchange Server needs to update all references to the tree. Click Yes when prompted to allow the update to occur.

To copy a public folder tree, follow these steps:

1. In System Manager, right-click the public folder tree you want to work with, and then select Copy.

2. In the administrative group node in which you want to create the tree, right-click Folders, and then select Paste.

3. You'll see a prompt that says the tree isn't unique within the Exchange organization. Click OK.

4. Type a new name for the tree, and then click OK. Exchange Server creates the new tree.

To move a public folder tree, follow these steps:

1. In System Manager, right-click the public folder tree you want to work with, and then select Cut.

2. Expand a different administrative group. Right-click Folders in this group, and then select Paste.

3. Moving the tree changes the directory path to the tree and as a result, the tree may become disconnected from the store it's associated with. When you click on it in System Manager, you'll see an error stating that the tree is no longer available.

4. To reconnect the tree with its store, right-click the tree, and then select Connect To. In the Select A Public Store dialog box, select the store that the tree should be connected to, and then click OK.

Deleting Public Folder Trees and Their Containers

You can delete public folder trees only when they contain no other objects and aren't associated with a public folder store. So before you try to delete a public folder tree, you must delete the other objects it contains as well as the public folder store in which it's placed. Afterward, you can delete the tree in System Manager by right-clicking it, and then selecting Delete. When prompted, confirm the deletion by clicking Yes.

Similarly, you can delete public folder containers only when they contain no other objects. Once you empty the container, you delete the container in System Manager by right-clicking it, and then selecting Delete. When prompted, confirm the deletion by clicking Yes.

Caution   You can't recover a public folder tree or container once it has been deleted. You can, however, restore the tree or container from backup. To do this, you'll need to restore the administrative group where the tree or container was created (which may overwrite changes to other items in the administrative group). See Chapter 10 for more information.

Creating and Adding Items to Public Folders

The following sections examine techniques you can use to create public folders within public folder trees. Keep in mind that while the Public Folders tree is accessible to MAPI clients, Windows applications, and Web browsers, other trees have limited accessibility.

Creating Public Folders in System Manager

Administrators can create public folders within public folder trees in several ways. One key way is to create the necessary folders in System Manager. To do that, complete the following steps:

1. Start System Manager. If administrative groups are enabled, expand Administrative Groups, and then expand the group you want to work with.

2. Expand Folders. Right-click the public folder tree in which you want to create the public folder, point to New, and then click Public Folder. You'll see a Properties dialog box.

3. Type a name for the public folder in the Name field, and then enter a description in the Public Folder Description field. The name you specify is used to set the e-mail address for the public folder. You can use the e-mail address to submit messages to the public folder.

4. Click the Replication tab, as shown in Figure 9-2. The Replicate Content To These Public Stores field lists the default public store for the public folder tree. To replicate the folder to other servers in the Exchange organization, click Add, select an additional public folder store to use, and then click OK. Repeat this process for other servers that should have replicas.

5. Replication message priority determines how items placed in folders are replicated. The available priorities are

   - **Urgent**   Messages in folders with Urgent priority are replicated before messages with other priorities, which can reduce delays in updating folders. Use this priority setting judiciously. Too many folders with urgent priority can degrade performance in the Exchange organization.

   - **Normal**   Messages in folders with Normal priority are sent before messages with Not Urgent priority. This is the default replication priority.

   - **Not Urgent**   Messages in folders with this priority are sent after messages with higher priority. Use this priority when items have low importance.

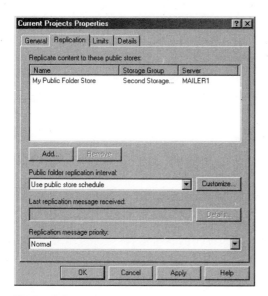

Figure 9-2. *To ensure that the folder is highly available, use the Replication tab to configure folder replication.*

6. In the Limits tab, select Use Public Store Defaults in each instance or enter specific defaults as described in the section of this chapter entitled "Setting Limits on Individual Folders."

7. Click OK. Complete, as necessary, the following tasks as explained in the section of this chapter entitled "Managing Public Folder Settings":

   - Set folder, message, and Active Directory rights
   - Designate public folder administrators
   - Propagate public folder settings

Creating Public Folders in Microsoft Outlook

Both administrators and authorized users can create public folders in Outlook. To do this, complete the following steps:

1. Start Outlook 2000. If the Folder List isn't displayed, click View, and then select Folder List.

2. Expand Public Folders in the Folder List, and then right-click All Public Folders or the top-level folder in which you want to place the public folder.

3. Select New Folder. You'll see the Create New Folder dialog box.

4. Enter a name for the public folder, and then use the Folder Contains drop-down list to choose the type of item you want to place in the folder.

5. Click OK. Complete, as necessary, the following tasks as explained in the section of this chapter entitled "Managing Public Folder Settings":

- Control replication and set messaging limits
- Set client permissions and Active Directory rights
- Designate public folder administrators
- Propagate public folder settings

Creating Public Folders in Internet Explorer

If a public folder tree is configured for Web sharing, administrators and authorized users can create public folders through Internet Explorer. To do this, follow these steps:

1. In the Address field of Internet Explorer 5.0 or later, type the URL of the public folder tree, such as ***http://mymailserver/public.***

2. If prompted, type your network user name and password. Then click OK.

3. As shown in Figure 9-3, you should see a folder view in the browser window. Right-click Public Folders or the top-level folder in which you want to place the public folder.

4. Select New Folder. You'll see the Create New Folder-Web Page dialog box.

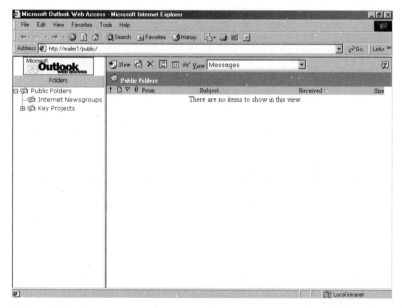

Figure 9-3. *You can use Internet Explorer to access public folders through Outlook Web Access. You'll find details on this feature in Chapter 13.*

5. Enter a name for the public folder, and then use the Folder Contains drop-down list to choose the type of item you want to place in the folder.

6. Click OK. Complete, as necessary, the following tasks as explained in the section of this chapter entitled "Managing Public Folder Settings":

   * Control replication and set messaging limits
   * Set client permissions and Active Directory rights
   * Designate public folder administrators
   * Propagate public folder settings

Adding Items to Public Folders

Authorized users can post items to public folders through any compliant application. Let's briefly look at how you could use Outlook 2000, Internet Explorer, and plain old e-mail to perform this task.

In Outlook 2000 authorized users can post items to public folders by completing these steps:

1. Start Outlook 2000. If the Folder List isn't displayed, click View, and then select Folder List.

2. Expand Public Folders in the Folder List, and then select the folder you want to use.

3. Click New or press CTRL+SHIFT+S. Notice that when a public folder is selected, the New button automatically changes to public folder post mode.

4. Type a subject for the message, and then type your message text. Add any necessary attachments.

5. Click Post.

In Internet Explorer, authorized users can post items to public folders by completing the following steps:

1. In the Address field of Internet Explorer 5.0 or later, type the URL of the public folder tree, such as ***http://mymailserver/public.***

2. If prompted, type your network user name and password. Then click OK.

3. In the Folders view, select the folder you want to use, and then click New.

4. Type a subject for the message, and then type your message text. Add any necessary attachments.

5. Click Post.

All public folders are mail-enabled by default. Mail-enabling allows authorized users to submit items using standard e-mail. Simply address an e-mail to the public folder and the message will be received as a posting. The default e-mail address is the same as the folder name (with any spaces or special characters removed). Administrators can check the e-mail address for a public folder by completing the following steps:

1. Start System Manager. If administrative groups are enabled, expand Administrative Groups, and then expand the group you want to work with.

2. Expand Folders, and then expand the public folder tree that contains the public folder you want to examine.

3. Right-click the public folder, and then select Properties. You'll see a Properties dialog box.

4. The folder's e-mail addresses are displayed in the E-mail Addresses tab. Note the SMTP (Simple Mail Transfer Protocol) address, because this is the one most e-mail clients will use.

Managing Public Folder Settings

You should actively manage public folders. If you don't, you won't get optimal performance, and users may encounter problems when reading from or posting to the folders. Each folder in a public folder tree has its own settings and each time a folder is created you should review and modify the following settings:

- Replication options
- Messaging limits
- Client permissions
- Active Directory rights

You may also want to designate folder administrators and propagate the changes you've made. This section of the chapter explains these and other public folder administration tasks.

Controlling Folder Replication

Each folder in a public folder tree has its own replication settings. By default, the content of a public folder is replicated only to the default public store for the tree. You can replicate the folder to additional public stores by following these steps:

1. Start System Manager. If administrative groups are enabled, expand Administrative Groups, and then expand the group you want to work with.

2. Expand Folders, and then expand the public folder tree that contains the public folder you want to replicate.

3. Right-click the public folder, and then select Properties.

4. Click the Replication tab. The Replicate Content To These Public Stores field shows where replicas of the folders are currently being created.

5. To replicate the folder to other servers in the Exchange organization, click Add, select an additional public folder store to use, and then click OK. Repeat this step for other servers that should have replicas.

6. The replication interval determines when changes to public folders are replicated. Use the Public Folder Replication Interval selection menu to choose a replication time. You can use a custom schedule by selecting Use Custom Schedule, clicking Customize, and then creating your custom schedule. You can use the public store's settings by selecting Use Public Store Schedule.

7. The replication priority determines how items placed in folders are replicated. The available priorities are Urgent, Normal, and Not Urgent. Messages in folders with a higher priority are replicated before messages in other folders.

8. Click OK.

Tip In most cases, you'll want to use the normal priority, which is the default. However, if a folder contains items that need to be replicated quickly throughout the organization, you may want to use the Urgent priority setting. Watch out though—too many folders with urgent priority can degrade performance in the Exchange organization.

Setting Limits on Individual Folders

In most cases you'll want to set storage limits and deleted item retention on a per store basis rather than on individual folders. If this is the case, see the section of Chapter 8 entitled "Setting Public Store Limits." On the other hand, if you want to set a limit on an individual folder, follow these steps:

1. Start System Manager. If administrative groups are enabled, expand Administrative Groups, and then expand the group you want to work with.

2. Expand Folders, and then expand the public folder tree that contains the public folder you want to replicate.

3. Right-click the public folder, and then select Properties.

4. Click the Limits tab. If you want to set storage limits on the folder, clear the Use Public Store Defaults check box in the Storage Limits panel, and then configure these options:

   * **Issue Warning At (KB)** Sets the size, in kilobytes, of the data that a user can post to the public folder before a warning is issued to the user. The warning tells the user to clean out the public folder.

   * **Prohibit Post At (KB)** Sets the maximum size, in kilobytes, of the data that the user can post to the public folder. The restriction ends when the total size of the user's data is under the limit.

   * **Maximum Item Size (KB)** Sets the maximum size, in kilobytes, for postings to the public folder.

5. If you want to set deleted item retention separately for the folder, clear the Use Public Store Defaults check box in the Deletion Settings panel, and then use Keep Deleted Items For (Days) to set the number of days to retain deleted items. An average retention period is 14 days. If you set the retention period to 0, deleted postings aren't retained and you can't recover them.

6. If you want to set age limits separately for the folder, clear the Use Public Store Defaults check box in the Age Limits panel, and then use Age Limit For Replicas (Days) to set the number of days to retain postings distributed to other servers.

7. Click OK.

Setting Client Permissions

You use client permissions to specify users who can access a particular public folder. By default, all users (including those accessing the folder anonymously over the Web) have permission to access the folder and read its contents. Users who log on to the network or to Outlook Web Access have additional permissions. These permissions allow them to create subfolders, to create items in the folder, to read items in the folder, and to edit and delete items they've created.

To change permissions for anonymous and authenticated users, you need to set a new role for the special users Anonymous and Default, respectively. Initially, anonymous users have the role of Contributor and authenticated users have the role of Publishing Author. These and other client permission roles are defined as follows:

- **Owner**   Grants all permissions in the folder. Users with this role can create, read, modify, and delete all items in the folder. They can create subfolders and can change permission on folders as well.

- **Publishing Editor**   Grants permission to create, read, modify, and delete all items in the folder. Users with this role can create subfolders as well.

- **Editor**   Grants permission to create, read, modify, and delete all items in the folder.

- **Publishing Author**   Grants permission to create and read items in the folder, to modify and delete items the user created, and to create subfolders.

- **Author**   Grants permission to create and read items in the folder as well as to modify and delete items that the user created.

- **Nonediting Author**   Grants permission to create and read items in the folder.

- **Reviewer**   Grants read-only permission.

- **Contributor**   Grants permission to create items but not to view the contents of the folder.

- **None**   Grants no permission in the folder.

To set new roles for users or to modify existing client permissions, complete the following steps:

1. Start System Manager. If administrative groups are enabled, expand Administrative Groups, and then expand the group you want to work with.

2. Expand Folders, and then expand the public folder tree that contains the public folder you want to replicate.

3. Right-click the public folder, and then select Properties.

4. On the Permissions tab, click Client Permissions. You'll see the Client Permissions dialog box shown in Figure 9-4.

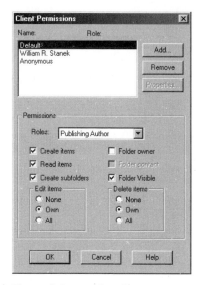

Figure 9-4. *Use the Client Permissions dialog box to set permissions for users, and then assign a role to each user. The role controls the actions the user can perform.*

5. The Name and Role lists display account names and their permissions on the folder. If you want to grant users permissions that are different from the default permission, click Add.

6. In the Add Users dialog box, select the name of a user who needs access to the mailbox. Then click Add to put the name on the Add Users list. Repeat this step as necessary for other users. Click OK when you're finished.

7. In the Name and Role lists, select one or more users whose permissions you want to modify. Then use the Roles selection list to assign a role or select individual permission items.

8. When you're finished granting permissions, click OK.

Setting Active Directory Rights and Designating Administrators

Client permissions allow users to manipulate folder contents, but they don't let users manage the permissions on the folder itself. Only administrators can set folder permissions and only administrators can modify public folder properties. If you want other users to be able to set permissions, grant the users directory rights to the folder. If you want users to be able to administer a public folder as well, grant them administrative rights to the folder.

To set a folder's directory and administrative rights, follow these steps:

1. Start System Manager. If administrative groups are enabled, expand Administrative Groups, and then expand the group you want to work with.

2. Expand Folders, and then expand the public folder tree that contains the public folder you want to replicate.

3. Right-click the public folder, and then select Properties.

4. On the Permissions tab, click Directory Rights, and then use the Permissions dialog box to set the folder's Active Directory permissions as described in the section of Chapter 6 entitled "Controlling Exchange Server Administration and Usage."

5. When you're finished setting directory rights, click Administrative Rights on the Permissions tab. Then use the Permissions dialog box to grant or deny administrative privileges.

6. Click OK when you're finished modifying the folder's rights.

Propagating Public Folder Settings

Any property changes you make to public folders aren't automatically applied to subfolders. You can, however, manually propagate setting changes if you need to. To do this, follow these steps:

1. Right-click the public folder whose settings you want to propagate to subfolders, point to All Tasks, and then click Propagate Settings.

2. You'll see the Propagate Folder Settings dialog box shown in Figure 9-5. Select the type of settings you want to propagate, and then click OK.

3. Exchange Server performs any necessary preparatory tasks, and then propagates the settings you've designated.

Viewing and Changing Address Settings for Public Folders

All public folders are mail-enabled by default and have the following characteristics that you can access in the folder's Properties dialog box:

- **An address list name** Set by default to be same as the folder name but not displayed in the Global Address List. You can set a new name with the Use This Name field found on the General tab. You can reveal the folder in the address list by clearing Hide From Exchange Address Lists on the Exchange Advanced tab.

- **An Exchange Server alias** Set by default to the name of the public folder. You can view and change it by using the Alias field on the Exchange General tab.

- **One or more e-mail addresses** Set by default for SMTP and X.400. Viewable and changeable in the E-mail Addresses tab.

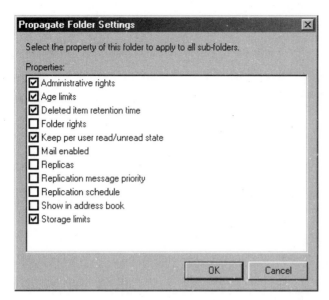

Figure 9-5. *The Propagate Folder Settings dialog box gives you complete control over the settings that are propagated to subfolders. Be sure to consider the impact of your changes before clicking OK.*

- **A display name**   Not set by default, but you can configure it by using the Simple Display Name field on the Exchange Advanced tab.

- **Delivery options**   Set by clicking the Delivery Options button on the Exchange General tab. Delivery options are covered in the sections of Chapter 4 entitled "Allowing Others to Access a Mailbox" and "Forwarding E-Mail to a New Address."

Manipulating, Renaming, and Recovering Public Folders

Because public folders are stored as objects in Active Directory, you can manipulate the folders using standard techniques, such as cut, copy, and paste. Follow the procedures outlined in this section to manipulate, rename, and recover public folders.

Renaming Public Folders

To rename a public folder, follow these steps:

1. In System Manager, right-click the public folder you want to rename.
2. Select Rename, type a new name, and then press ENTER.

Copying and Moving Public Folders

You can copy and move public folders only within the same public folder tree. You can't copy or move a public folder to a different tree.

To create a copy of a public folder, follow these steps:

1. In System Manager, right-click the public folder you want to work with, and then select Copy.

2. Right-click the folder into which you want to copy the folder, and then select Paste.

To move a public folder to a new location in the same tree, follow these steps:

1. In System Manager, right-click the public folder you want to work with, and then select Cut.

2. Right-click the folder into which you want to move the folder, and then select Paste.

Deleting Public Folders

When you delete a public folder, you remove its contents, any subfolders it contains, and the contents of its subfolders. Before you delete a folder, however, you should ensure that any existing data the folder contains is no longer needed and make a backup of the folder contents just in case.

You delete public folders and their subfolders by completing the following steps:

1. In System Manager, right-click the public folder you want to remove, and then select Delete.

2. You'll be asked to confirm the action. Click Yes.

Recovering Public Folders

You can recover deleted folders from public folder stores, provided you've set a deleted item retention period for the public folder store from which the folders were deleted and the retention period for this data store hasn't expired. If both of these are the case, you can recover deleted folders by completing the following steps:

1. Log on to the domain using an account with administrative privileges in the domain or with an account with full control over the public folders you need to recover.

2. After starting Outlook 2000, access the Public Folders node, and then select the All Public Folders node or the node that contained the public folders.

3. From the Tools menu, select Recover Deleted Items. You should now see the Recover Deleted Items From dialog box.

4. Select the folder(s) you want to recover, and then click Recover Selected Items.

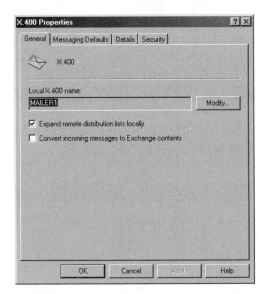

Figure 12-1. *Use the General tab of the X.400 Properties dialog box to set the Local X.400 Name and other message options.*

Expanding Remote Distribution Lists and Converting Messages

The X.400 MTA has limited control over how incoming messages are handled. You can configure whether remote distribution lists are expanded and whether incoming messages are converted to Exchange contents.

Expanding remote distribution lists makes the lists available to users on the local server. This is the optimal setting and is enabled by default. Only in rare circumstances, when you want to expand lists elsewhere, should you disable this option.

Converting incoming messages changes the message addressing and contents to a form compatible with Exchange and Messaging Application Programming Interface (MAPI) clients. If you experience problems with message addressing from foreign systems, you may want to enable this option temporarily to see if this resolves the problem. Otherwise, this option is usually disabled.

To change these messaging settings, follow these steps:

1. Start System Manager. If Administrative Groups are enabled, expand the administrative group in which the server you want to use is located.

2. Navigate to the X.400 container in the console tree. Expand Servers, expand the server you want to work with, and then expand Protocols.

3. Right-click X.400, and then select Properties. This displays the X.400 Properties dialog box shown in Figure 12-1.

4. Select Expand Remote Distribution Lists Locally to make remote lists available. Or clear this field to disable this option.

5. Select Convert Incoming Messages To Exchange Contents to convert incoming message contents. Or clear this field to disable this option.

6. Click OK.

Setting Connection Retry Values for X.400

Connection retry values for the X.400 MTA play a key role in determining how Exchange Server connects to other servers and how messages are transferred. Retry values do not, however, control message delivery. Message delivery is controlled by the messaging protocol.

You can configure four message retry values. These values are:

- **Maximum Open Retries** Controls the maximum number of times Exchange Server tries to open a connection before failing and generating a nondelivery report. The default is 144 retries.

- **Open Interval** Controls the number of seconds Exchange Server waits before attempting to reopen a failed connection. The default is 600 seconds.

- **Maximum Transfer Retries** Controls the maximum number of times Exchange Server tries to transfer a message across an open connection before failing and generating a nondelivery report. The default is two retries.

- **Transfer Interval** Controls the number of seconds Exchange Server waits before attempting to resend a message across an open connection. The default is 120 seconds.

Based on these values, a typical connection looks like this:

1. Exchange Server attempts to open a connection to the destination mail system. If it's unable to establish a connection, Exchange Server waits for the open interval and then tries to open a connection again—as long as the maximum retry value hasn't been reached. If the maximum retry value has been reached, Exchange Server generates a nondelivery report that gets returned to the sender.

2. Once a connection has been established, Exchange Server attempts to transfer the message. If it's unable to transfer the message, Exchange Server waits for the transfer interval and then tries to transfer the message again—as long as the maximum retry value hasn't been reached. If the maximum retry value has been reached, Exchange Server generates a nondelivery report that gets returned to the sender.

To view or change connection retry values for the X.400 MTA, follow these steps:

1. Start System Manager. If Administrative Groups are enabled, expand the administrative group in which the server you want to use is located.

2. Navigate to the X.400 container in the console tree. Expand Servers, expand the server you want to work with, and then expand Protocols.

3. Right-click X.400, and then select Properties. This displays the X.400 Properties dialog box shown in Figure 12-1.

4. Click the Messaging Defaults tab. You'll see the current connection retry values. You can enter new values or click Reset Default Value to restore the default connection values.

5. Click OK.

Note The default connection retry values are less than optimal in many situations, and you can often improve the performance of Exchange Server by adjusting these values for your environment.

Setting RTS Values for X.400

Reliable transfer service (RTS) values for the X.400 MTA play a key role in determining how Exchange Server transfers message data. You can configure three RTS values. These values are:

- **Checkpoint Size (KB)**   Controls the amount of data Exchange Server transfers before performing a checkpoint. If the checkpoint results in an error being generated, Exchange Server restarts the message transfer from the most recent checkpoint. The default value is 15 KB.

- **Recovery Timeout (Sec)**   Controls the amount of time Exchange Server waits for a broken connection to be reestablished. If the wait exceeds the timeout value, Exchange Server restarts the message transfer. The default value is 60 seconds.

- **Window Size**   Controls the maximum number of unacknowledged checkpoints that can occur. If this value is exceeded, message transfer is suspended. The default is five.

Based on these values, a typical data transfer looks like this:

1. Exchange Server begins transferring data across an open connection. The transfer continues until a checkpoint is reached. After performing a checkpoint (and assuming an error didn't occur), Exchange Server continues the data transfer.

2. If the checkpoint is acknowledged, Exchange Server resets a counter tracking the current window size against the maximum value allowable. If the checkpoint isn't acknowledged, Exchange Server increments the tracking counter. Anytime the value of the counter exceeds the maximum allowable window size, an error occurs.

3. If an error is generated at the checkpoint, the transfer stops and Exchange Server waits for the recovery timeout interval before restarting the message transfer from the most recent checkpoint that was acknowledged.

To view or change RTS values for the X.400 MTA, follow these steps:

1. Start System Manager. If Administrative Groups are enabled, expand the administrative group in which the server you want to use is located.

2. Navigate to the X.400 container in the console tree. Expand Servers, expand the server you want to work with, and then expand Protocols.

3. Right-click X.400, and then select Properties.

4. Click the Messaging Defaults tab, and then click Additional Values. As shown in Figure 12-2, the RTS Values panel displays the current RTS values. You can enter new values as necessary or click Reset Default Values to restore the default settings for RTS, association parameters, and transfer timeouts.

> **Tip** If you have an unreliable connection, you may want to decrease the checkpoint size, which forces Exchange Server to perform checkpoints more frequently. However, you should rarely (if ever) set the checkpoint size to zero. Setting the checkpoint size to zero tells Exchange Server not to perform checkpoints and, as a result, message transfer may become unreliable.

5. Click OK.

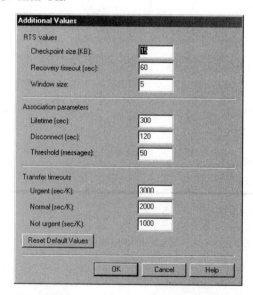

Figure 12-2. *Use the Additional Values dialog box to configure RTS values, association parameters, and transfer timeouts.*

Setting Association Parameters for X.400

Association parameters for the X.400 MTA play a key role in determining how Exchange Server handles connections once they've been established. You can configure three association parameters. These values are:

- **Lifetime (Sec)**   Controls the amount of time Exchange Server maintains an association for a remote system. A key property of the association is the identification of an open connection to a remote system. If the lifetime expires, the association is terminated but the related connection isn't broken until the disconnect period expires. The default value is 300 seconds.

- **Disconnect (Sec)**   Controls the amount of time Exchange Server waits before disconnecting a connection that no longer has an association. Typically, you want connections to remain open for a short period after the association is terminated. The default is 120 seconds.

- **Threshold (Messages)**   Controls the maximum queue size for each association. When the number of queued messages for the association exceeds this value, Exchange Server establishes a new connection and creates a new association. The default is 50 messages.

Here's how Exchange Server uses these values to handle open connections:

1. Exchange Server creates an association for each open connection to a remote system. It creates new associations as new messages enter the queue and new connections are established. It also creates new associations when the number of queued messages to any single remote server exceeds the threshold value.

2. When there are no more messages to send to a particular remote server, Exchange Server starts tracking the association lifetime. If the lifetime expires, the association is terminated but the connection remains open.

3. The open connection to the server isn't broken automatically. If a new message is queued for a server whose association was terminated and the connection is still open, Exchange Server creates a new association and transfers the message. Otherwise, the open connection is broken when the disconnect value is reached.

You can view or change association parameters for the X.400 MTA by completing the following steps:

1. Start System Manager. If Administrative Groups are enabled, expand the administrative group in which the server you want to use is located.

2. Navigate to the X.400 container in the console tree. Expand Servers, expand the server you want to work with, and then expand Protocols.

3. Right-click X.400, and then select Properties.

4. Click the Messaging Defaults tab, and then click Additional Values. The Association Parameters panel displays the current parameters. You can enter new values as necessary or click Reset Default Values to restore the default settings for RTS, association parameters, and transfer timeouts.

5. Click OK.

Setting Transfer Timeout for X.400

Generating lots of nondelivery reports in a short amount of time can seriously degrade the performance of Exchange Server. To prevent this from happening, Exchange Server doesn't immediately generate nondelivery reports. Instead, Exchange Server generates the nondelivery report based on the message priority, the associated transfer timeout value, and the size of the message. The default transfer timeout values are

- **Urgent** 3000 seconds per KB
- **Normal** 2000 seconds per KB
- **Not Urgent** 1000 seconds per KB

 Note At first glance, the default values seem reversed. But you'd logically want to allow longer transfer times for urgent messages and shorter transfer times for less important messages. More time may ensure that an important message makes it across an unreliable link.

You can view or change transfer timeouts for the X.400 MTA by completing the following steps:

1. Start System Manager. If Administrative Groups are enabled, expand the administrative group in which the server you want to use is located.

2. Navigate to the X.400 container in the console tree. Expand Servers, expand the server you want to work with, and then expand Protocols.

3. Right-click X.400, and then select Properties.

4. Click the Messaging Defaults tab, and then click Additional Values. The Transfer Timeouts panel displays the current parameters. You can enter new values as necessary or click Reset Default Values to restore the default settings for RTS, association parameters, and transfer timeouts.

5. Click OK.

Using Routing Group Connectors

Routing group connectors are the easiest connectors to configure and, as such, they're the preferred connectors for Exchange Server. You use a routing group connector to link two routing groups. These routing groups must be within the same organization. For those of you familiar with previous versions of Exchange Server, this concept is similar to a Site Connector.

Understanding Routing Group Connectors

Routing group connectors establish links between routing groups using one or more designated bridgehead servers. Bridgehead servers act as communication relays for routing groups and you define them both locally and remotely.

Local bridgehead servers serve as the originator of message traffic, and remote bridgehead servers serve as the destination for message traffic. By default, all servers in the originating routing group act as local bridgehead servers. You can, however, select specific servers to act as bridgeheads. Selecting multiple servers as local bridgeheads provides load balancing and fault tolerance, which is essential when high availability is a concern. Selecting a single server as the local bridgehead ensures that all mail flows through the designated server, but it doesn't provide redundancy.

For the routing group connector, delivery options control when messages are sent through the connector. One of the key features is your ability to set connection schedules for all messages or specifically for standard-sized and large-sized messages. If you have a relatively fast and reliable link between the two routing groups, you probably want to set the same delivery schedule for all messages. On the other hand, if you have a relatively slow link between the two routing groups, you may want to set a separate schedule for large messages to ensure that oversized messages don't take all the available bandwidth during peak usage hours.

The routing group connector can deliver messages at many intervals. The interval you use depends on your reliability and availability needs:

- If you want message delivery to be highly reliable and the link to be highly available, you probably want to set the delivery interval to Always Run or Run Every Hour. You may also want to set a custom schedule that has an interval of every 30 minutes.

- If you want message delivery to be reliable and available but don't want message delivery to be a priority, you probably want to set the delivery interval to Run Every Two Hours or Run Every Four Hours.

- If the link is used to distribute message digests or public folder data infrequently, you probably want to set a specific delivery time, such as Run Daily At 11:00 P.M., Run Daily At 12:00 A.M., Run Daily At 1:00 A.M., or Run Daily At 2:00 A.M.

Installing Routing Group Connectors

To install a routing group connector, complete the following steps:

1. Start System Manager. If Administrative Groups are enabled, expand the administrative group you want to work with.

2. To install a routing group connector, you must have at least two routing groups in the organization. Expand Routing Groups, and then expand the routing group you want to use as the originator of the connection.

3. Right-click Connectors, click New, and then choose Routing Group Connector. This displays the dialog box shown in Figure 12-3.

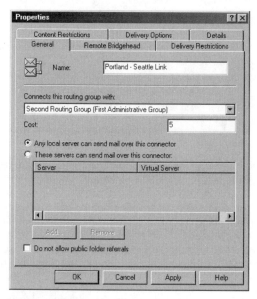

Figure 12-3. *Use the Routing Group Connector Properties dialog box to configure connectivity between two routing groups.*

4. In the General tab, type a descriptive name for the connector.

5. Choose the destination routing group by selecting it in the Connect This Routing Group With list box.

6. If you want all servers in the originating routing group to act as bridgehead servers, select Any Local Server Can Send Mail Over This Connector. Otherwise, select These Servers Can Send Mail Over This Connector, and then designate the local bridgehead servers that you want to use by clicking Add, and then selecting servers from the list provided.

7. In the Remote Bridgehead tab, click Add. You'll see a list of available routing groups and servers. In the destination routing group, select the server that you want to act as the remote bridgehead.

8. Click OK to install the connector. Later, you may want to set connector cost, delivery options, delivery restrictions, and content restrictions.

Configuring Routing Group Connector Delivery Options

To set the delivery options for an existing routing group connector, follow these steps:

1. Start System Manager. If Administrative Groups are enabled, expand the administrative group you want to work with.

2. To install a routing group connector, you must have at least two routing groups in your organization. Expand Routing Groups, and then expand the routing group you want to use as the originator of the connection.

3. Expand Connectors, right-click the routing group connector you want to configure, and then select Properties.

4. Click the Delivery Options tab, as shown in Figure 12-4. Use the Connection Time list box to specify the times when messages are sent through the connector. The available options are: Always Run, Run Daily At 11:00 P.M., Run Daily At 12:00 A.M., Run Daily At 1:00 A.M., Run Daily At 2:00 A.M., Run Every Hour, Run Every 2 Hours, Run Every 4 Hours, Never Run, and Use Custom Schedule.

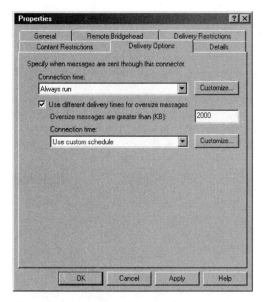

Figure 12-4. *Use the Delivery Options tab to control when messages are sent through the routing group connector.*

5. To set separate delivery options for standard and large messages, select Use Different Delivery Times For Oversize Messages. In Oversize Messages Are Greater Than (KB), type the minimum size, in kilobytes, of messages you want to designate as oversized. The default is 2000 KB. Finally, use the options in the second Connection Time list box to set the delivery times for large messages.

6. Click OK.

Performing Other Routing Group Connector Tasks

You perform most other routing group connector tasks in the same way that you perform tasks for other connectors. The section of this chapter entitled "Handling Core Connector Administration Tasks" explains these common tasks.

Using SMTP Connectors

SMTP connectors are another type of Exchange connector. SMTP connectors transfer messages from local bridgehead servers to remote servers. You use SMTP connectors to connect Exchange servers, non-Exchange servers, routing groups, and organizations.

Understanding SMTP Connectors

SMTP connectors are a bit more complex than routing group connectors, but the additional settings they make available gives them definite advantages over routing group connectors. With SMTP connectors, you can encrypt message traffic sent over the link and require stricter authentication than with routing group connectors. You can transmit messages to a designated server—called a *smart host*, which then transfers the message—or you can use Domain Name System (DNS) mail exchanger (MX) records to route messages. If the other mail system supports Extension to SMTP (ESMTP), you can enable extended options as well.

When you install an SMTP connector, you must define which local bridgehead servers the connector will use as well as the connector scope, message routing technique, and address space. SMTP virtual servers act as local bridgehead servers for SMTP connectors. This means that the virtual servers are responsible for routing the message traffic. Multiple local bridgeheads provide load balancing and fault tolerance, which is essential when high availability is a concern. A single bridgehead, on the other hand, ensures that all mail flows through a designated server, but it doesn't provide redundancy.

SMTP connectors have a specific scope that controls how the connector routes messages. You use an SMTP connector with a routing group scope to transfer messages within your organization. You can use an SMTP connector with an organizational scope to connect independent Exchange organizations, to connect Exchange servers with other SMTP-compatible servers (such as Unix Sendmail servers), and to connect Exchange 2000 Server with earlier versions of Exchange Server.

SMTP connectors use smart hosts or DNS MX records to route mail. If you use a smart host, Exchange 2000 Server transfers messages directly to the smart host, which then sends out messages over an established link. The smart host allows you to route messages on a per domain basis. If you use DNS MX records, Exchange 2000 Server performs a DNS lookup for each address to which the connector sends mail.

When you install an SMTP connector, you must also define the address space for the connector. The address space determines when the connector is used. For example, if you want to connect two domains in the same Exchange organization—*dev.microsoft.com* and *corp.microsoft.com*—you could create the SMTP connector in *dev.microsoft.com*, and then add an SMTP address type for the e-mail domain *corp.microsoft.com*.

You can define multiple address types for a single SMTP connector. The address types can be any combination of SMTP, X.400, MS Mail, cc:Mail, Lotus Notes, and Lotus GroupWise addresses. These address types can point to different domains. Thus, you could use an SMTP connector to connect *dev.microsoft.com* with *sales.microsoft.com, bizdev.microsoft.com,* and *eng.microsoft.com.* You could also use an SMTP connector to connect two specific routing groups.

For load balancing and high availability, you could configure multiple SMTP connectors to handle the same address space. For example, if a large volume of traffic is routinely sent between *corp.microsoft.com* and *support.microsoft.com*, you could install two SMTP connectors to handle the message routing between these domains.

Installing SMTP Connectors

To install an SMTP connector, complete the following steps:

1. Start System Manager. If administrative groups are enabled, expand the administrative group you want to work with.

2. If available, expand Routing Groups, and then expand the routing group you want to use as the originator of the connection.

3. Right-click Connectors, click New, and then choose SMTP Connector. This displays the dialog box shown in Figure 12-5.

4. In the General tab, type a descriptive name for the connector.

5. To use a smart host for routing, select Forward All Mail Through This Connector To The Following Smart Host, and then type the fully qualified domain name or IP address of the server through which you'd like to route messages. The SMTP connector then uses this smart host to route messages to the remote server.

Tip If you use an IP address, be sure to enclose the address in brackets, such as [192.168.12.99]. The brackets tell Exchange Server that the value is an IP address and, as a result, Exchange Server doesn't try to perform a DNS lookup on the value.

Chapter 13

Administering SMTP, IMAP4, and POP3

Microsoft Exchange 2000 Server supports Simple Mail Transfer Protocol (SMTP), Internet Message Access Protocol 4 (IMAP4), and Post Office Protocol 3 (POP3). These protocols play an important role in determining how mail is delivered and transferred both within and outside the Exchange organization.

- SMTP is the native mail protocol for mail submission and mail transport. This means that clients use SMTP to send messages and Exchange servers use SMTP to deliver messages and message data.
- IMAP4 is a protocol for reading mail and accessing public folders on remote servers. Clients can log on to an Exchange server and use IMAP4 to download message headers and then read messages individually while online.
- POP3 is a protocol for retrieving mail on remote servers. Clients can log on to an Exchange server and then use POP3 to download their mail for offline use.

Each of these protocols has an associated virtual server. You use virtual servers to specify configuration information and to control access. You can create additional virtual servers as well.

The following sections examine the key tasks you'll use to manage SMTP, IMAP4, and POP3.

Working with SMTP, IMAP4, and POP3 Virtual Servers

SMTP, IMAP4, and POP3 services are hosted on separate virtual servers. A virtual server is a server process that has its own configuration information, which includes an IP address, a port number, and authentication settings. If you installed SMTP, IMAP4, and POP3 using the default options:

- The default SMTP virtual server is configured to use any available IP address on the server and respond on port 25. SMTP virtual servers replace and extend the Internet Mail Connector (IMC) and Internet Mail Service (IMS) that were used in previous versions of Exchange Server. To control outbound connections and message delivery, you configure the default SMTP virtual server for the organization.

- The default IMAP4 virtual server is configured to use any available IP address on the server and respond on ports 143 and 993. Port 143 is used for standard communications, and port 993 is used for Secure Sockets Layer (SSL) communications. IMAP4 virtual servers allow Internet clients to download message headers and then read messages individually while online.

- The default POP3 virtual server is configured to use any available IP address on the server and respond on ports 110 and 995. Port 110 is used for standard communications, and port 995 is used for SSL communications. POP3 virtual servers allow Internet clients to download mail for offline use.

You can change the IP address and port assignment at any time. In most cases you'll want the messaging protocol to respond on a specific IP address. For SMTP, this is the IP address or addresses you've designated in the Domain Name System (DNS) mail exchanger records for the domains you're supporting through Exchange Server. For IMAP4 and POP3, this is the IP address or IP addresses associated with the fully qualified domain name of the Exchange servers providing these services.

While a single Exchange server could provide SMTP, IMAP4, and POP3 services, you can install these services on separate Exchange servers. Here are some typical scenarios:

- In a moderately sized enterprise, you may want one Exchange server to handle SMTP and another to handle IMAP4 and POP3. You install Server A as the SMTP server and then update the domain's mail exchanger (MX) record so that it points to Server A. Next, you install Server B as the POP3 and IMAP4 server. Afterward, you configure Internet mail clients so that they use Server B for POP3/IMAP4 (incoming mail) and Server A for SMTP (outgoing mail).

- In a large enterprise, you may want a different Exchange server for each protocol. You install Server A as the SMTP server and then update the domain's MX record so that it points to Server A. Next, you install Server B as the POP3 server and Server C as the IMAP4 server. Afterward, you configure POP3 clients so that they use Server B for POP3 (incoming mail) and Server A for SMTP (outgoing mail). Then you configure IMAP4 clients so that they use Server C for IMAP4 (incoming mail) and Server A for SMTP (outgoing mail).

- When mail exchange is critical to the enterprise, you may want to build fault tolerance into the Exchange organization. Typically, you do this by installing multiple Exchange servers that support each protocol. For example, to ensure fault tolerance for SMTP, you could install Server A, Server B, and Server C as SMTP servers. Then, when you create the domain's MX records, you set a priority of 10 for Server A, a priority of 20 for Server B, and a priority of 30 for Server C. In this way, any one of the servers can be offline without affecting mail submission and delivery in the organization.

A single virtual server can provide messaging services for multiple domains. You can also install multiple virtual servers of the same type. You can use additional virtual servers to help provide fault tolerance in a large enterprise or to handle messaging services for multiple domains. When you create multiple SMTP virtual servers, you must also create additional MX records for the servers.

Mastering Core SMTP, IMAP4, and POP3 Administration

Regardless of whether you're working with SMTP, IMAP4, or POP3, you'll perform a common set of administrative tasks. These tasks are examined in this section.

Starting, Stopping, and Pausing Virtual Servers

Virtual servers run under a server process, which you can start, stop, and pause much like other server processes. For example, if you're changing the configuration of a virtual server or performing other maintenance tasks, you may need to stop the virtual server, make the changes, and then restart it. When you stop a virtual server, it doesn't accept connections from users, and you can't use it to deliver or retrieve mail.

An alternative to stopping a virtual server is to pause it. Pausing a virtual server prevents new client connections, but it doesn't disconnect current connections. When you pause a POP3 or IMAP4 virtual server, active clients can continue to retrieve mail. When you pause an SMTP virtual server, active clients can continue to submit messages and the virtual server can deliver existing messages that are queued for delivery. No new connections are accepted, however.

The master process for all virtual servers is the Microsoft Windows 2000 service under which the virtual server process runs—either SMTP, Microsoft Exchange IMAP4, or Microsoft Exchange POP3. Stopping the master process stops all virtual servers using the process and halts all message delivery for the service. Starting the master process restarts all virtual servers that were running when the master process was stopped.

You can start, stop, or pause a virtual server by completing the following steps:

1. Start System Manager. If administrative groups are enabled, expand the administrative group in which the server you want to use is located.

2. In the console tree, navigate to the Protocols container. Expand Servers, expand the server you want to work with, and then expand Protocols.

3. In the console tree, expand SMTP, IMAP4, or POP3, and then right-click the virtual server you want to manage. You can now

   - Select Start to start the virtual server.
   - Select Stop to stop the virtual server.
   - Select Pause to pause the virtual server.

Note The *metabase update service* is responsible for processing and replicating configuration changes. This service reads data from Active Directory directory service and enters it into the virtual server's local metabase. Exchange Server uses the service to make configuration changes to virtual servers on remote systems without needing a permanent connection. When the service updates a remote server, it may need several minutes to read and apply the changes.

You can start, stop, or pause the master process for virtual servers by completing the following steps:

1. From the Administrative Tools program group, start Computer Management.

2. In the console tree, right-click the Computer Management entry, and from the shortcut menu, choose Connect To Another Computer. You can now choose the Exchange server whose services you want to manage.

3. Expand the Services And Applications node by clicking the plus sign (+) next to it, and then choose Services. The SMTP, Microsoft Exchange IMAP4, and Microsoft Exchange POP3 services control SMTP, IMAP4, and POP3, respectively.

4. Right-click the service you want to manipulate, and then select Start, Stop, or Pause as appropriate. You can also choose Restart to have Windows stop and then start the service after a brief pause. Also, if you pause a service, you can use the Resume option to resume normal operation.

Configuring Ports and IP Addresses Used by Virtual Servers

Each virtual server has an IP address and a TCP port configuration setting. The default IP address setting is to use any available IP address. On a multihomed server, however, you'll usually want messaging protocols to respond on a specific IP address and to do this, you need to change the default setting.

What the default port setting is depends on the messaging protocol being used and whether SSL is enabled or disabled. Table 13-1 shows the default port settings for key protocols used by Exchange 2000 Server.

Table 13-1. Standard and Secure Port Settings for Messaging Protocols

Protocol	Default Port	Default Secure Port
SMTP	25	
HTTP	80	443
IMAP4	143	993
POP3	110	995
NNTP (Network News Transfer Protocol)	119	563

To change the IP address or port number for a virtual server, complete the following steps:

1. Start System Manager. If administrative groups are enabled, expand the administrative group in which the server you want to use is located.

2. In the console tree, navigate to the Protocols container. Expand Servers, expand the server you want to work with, and then expand Protocols.

3. In the console tree, expand SMTP, IMAP4, or POP3. Right-click the virtual server you want to manage, and then select Properties.

4. In the General tab, use the IP Address selection list to select an available IP address. Select (All Unassigned) to allow the protocol to respond on all unassigned IP addresses that are configured on the server.

Tip   If the IP address you want to use isn't listed and you want the server to respond on that IP address, you'll need to update the server's TCP/IP network configuration. For details, see "Assigning a Static IP Address" in Chapter 15 of *Microsoft Windows 2000 Administrator's Pocket Consultant* (Microsoft Press, 2000).

5. In the General tab, click Advanced. As Figure 13-1 shows, the Advanced dialog box shows the current TCP port settings for the protocol. You can assign ports for individual IP addresses and for all unassigned IP addresses.

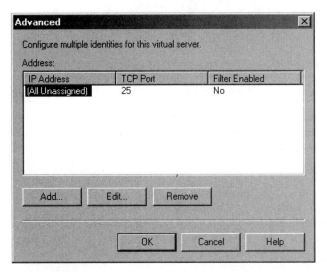

Figure 13-1. *Use the Advanced dialog box to configure TCP ports on an individual IP address basis or for all unassigned IP addresses.*

6. Use the following options in the Advanced dialog box to modify port settings:

- **Add** Adds a TCP port on a per IP address basis or all unassigned IP address basis. Click Add, and then select the IP address you want to use.

- **Edit** Allows you to edit the TCP port settings for the currently selected entry in the Address list box.

- **Remove** Allows you to remove the TCP port settings for the currently selected entry in the Address list box.

 Note The IP address/TCP port combination must be unique on every virtual server. Multiple virtual servers can use the same port as long as the servers are configured to use different IP addresses.

7. Click OK twice.

Controlling Incoming Connections to Virtual Servers

You can control incoming connections to virtual servers in several ways. You can

- Grant or deny access using IP addresses or Internet domain names.
- Require secure incoming connections.
- Require authentication for incoming connections.
- Restrict concurrent connections and set connection time-out values.

Each of these tasks is discussed in the sections that follow.

 Note With SMTP, you can configure both incoming and outbound connections. To learn how to configure outbound connections for SMTP, see the section of this chapter entitled "Configuring Outgoing Connections."

Securing Access by IP Address, Subnet, or Domain

By default, virtual servers are accessible to all IP addresses, which presents a security risk that may allow your messaging system to be misused. To control use of a virtual server, you may want to grant or deny access by IP address, subnet, or domain.

- Granting access allows a computer to access the virtual server but doesn't necessarily allow users to submit or retrieve messages. If you require authentication, users still need to authenticate themselves.

- Denying access prevents a computer from accessing the virtual server. As a result, users of the computer can't submit or retrieve messages from the virtual server—even if they could have authenticated themselves with a user name and password.

As stated earlier, POP3 and IMAP4 virtual servers control message retrieval by remote clients and SMTP virtual servers control message delivery. Thus, if you want to block users outside the organization from sending mail, you deny access to the SMTP virtual server. If you want to block users from retrieving mail, you deny access to POP3, IMAP4, or both.

Note   You can also restrict access by e-mail address. To do this, you must set a filter and then enable the filter on the SMTP virtual server. For details, see the section of Chapter 11 entitled "Setting Message Filters."

To grant or deny access to a virtual server by IP address, subnet, or domain, follow these steps:

1. Start System Manager. If administrative groups are enabled, expand the administrative group in which the server you want to use is located.
2. In the console tree, navigate to the Protocols container. Expand Servers, expand the server you want to work with, and then expand Protocols.
3. In the console tree, expand SMTP, IMAP4, or POP3. Right-click the virtual server you want to manage, and then select Properties.
4. Click Connection in the Access tab. As shown in Figure 13-2, the Computers list shows the computers that currently have connection controls.

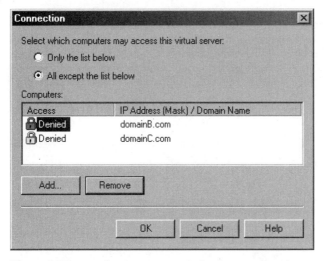

Figure 13-2. *Use the Connection dialog box to control connections by IP address, subnet, or domain.*

5. To grant access to specific computers and deny access to all others, click Only The List Below.
6. To deny access to specific computers and grant access to all others, click All Except The List Below.

7. Create the grant or deny list. Click Add, and then in the Computer dialog box specify Single Computer, Group Of Computers, or Domain.

- For a single computer, type the IP address for the computer, such as **192.168.5.50**.

- For groups of computers, type the subnet address, such as **192.168.5**, and the subnet mask, such as **255.255.0.0**.

- For a domain name, type the fully qualified domain name, such as **eng.domain.com**.

 Caution When you grant or deny by domain, Exchange Server must perform a reverse DNS lookup on each connection to determine whether the connection comes from the domain. These reverse lookups can severely affect Exchange Server's performance, and this performance impact increases as the number of concurrent users and connections increases.

8. If you want to remove an entry from the grant or deny list, select the related entry in the Computers list, and then click Remove.

9. Click OK.

Controlling Secure Communications for Incoming Connections

By default, mail clients pass connection information and message data through an insecure connection. If corporate security is a high priority, however, your information security team may require mail clients to connect over secure communication channels. You have several options for configuring secure communications including smart cards, SSL, and PGP. In an environment where you need to support multiple transfer protocols, such as HTTP and SMTP, SSL offers a good solution.

You configure secure SSL communications by completing the following steps:

1. Create a certificate request for the Exchange server that you want to use secure communications. Each server (but not necessarily each virtual server) must have its own certificate.

2. Submit the certificate request to a certificate authority (CA). The certificate authority will then issue you a certificate (usually for a fee).

3. Install the certificate on the Exchange server. Repeat Steps 1-3 for each Exchange server that needs to communicate over a secure channel.

4. Configure the server to require secure communications on a per virtual server basis.

Following this procedure, you could create, install, and enable a certificate for use on a virtual server by completing the following steps:

1. Start System Manager. If administrative groups are enabled, expand the administrative group in which the server you want to use is located.

2. In the console tree, navigate to the Protocols container. Expand Servers, expand the server you want to work with, and then expand Protocols.

3. In the console tree, expand SMTP, IMAP4, or POP3. Right-click the virtual server that you want to use secure communications, and then select Properties.

4. In the Access tab, click Certificate. This starts the Web Certificate Wizard. Use the wizard to create a new certificate. For additional virtual servers on the same Exchange server, you'll want to assign an existing certificate.

5. Send the certificate request to your certificate authority. When you receive the certificate back from the CA, access the Web Certificate Wizard from the virtual server's Properties dialog box again. Now you'll be able to process the pending request and install the certificate.

6. When you're finished installing the certificate, don't close the Properties dialog box. Instead, on the Access tab, click Communication.

7. In the Security dialog box, click Require Secure Channel. If you've also configured 128-bit security, select Require 128-bit Encryption.

8. Click OK twice.

Note   For worldwide installations, you'll want to use 40-bit encryption. The 128-bit encryption level is available only in the United States and Canada.

Controlling Authentication for Incoming Connections

Exchange 2000 Server supports two authentication methods:

- **Basic Authentication**   With basic authentication, users are prompted for logon information. When it's entered, this information is transmitted unencrypted across the network. If you've configured secure communications on the server as described in the section of this chapter entitled "Controlling Secure Communications for Incoming Connections," you can require clients to use SSL. When you use SSL with basic authentication, the logon information is encrypted before transmission.

- **Integrated Windows Authentication**   With integrated Windows authentication, Exchange Server uses standard Windows security to validate the user's identity. Instead of prompting for a user name and password, clients relay the logon credentials that users supply when they log on to Windows. These credentials are fully encrypted without the need for SSL, and they include the user name and password needed to log on to the network.

Both authentication methods are enabled by default for SMTP, IMAP4, and POP3. Because of this, the default logon process looks like this:

1. Exchange Server attempts to obtain the user's Windows credentials. If the credentials can be validated and the user has the appropriate access permissions, the user is allowed to log on to the virtual server.

2. If validation of the credentials fails or no credentials are available, the server uses basic authentication and tells the client to display a logon prompt. When

the logon information is submitted, the server validates the logon. If the credentials can be validated and the user has the appropriate access permissions, the user is allowed to log on to the virtual server.

3. If validation fails or the user doesn't have appropriate access permissions, the user is denied access to the virtual server.

As necessary, you can enable or disable support for these authentication methods. You can do that by completing the following steps:

1. Start System Manager. If administrative groups are enabled, expand the administrative group in which the server you want to use is located.

2. In the console tree, navigate to the Protocols container. Expand Servers, expand the server you want to work with, and then expand Protocols.

3. In the console tree, expand SMTP, IMAP4, or POP3. Right-click the virtual server that you want to work with, and then select Properties.

4. In the Access tab, click Authentication. This displays the Authentication dialog box shown in Figure 13-3.

Figure 13-3. *You can use the Authentication dialog box to enable or disable authentication methods to meet the needs of your organization. With basic authentication, it's often helpful to set a default domain as well.*

5. Select or clear Basic Authentication to enable or disable this authentication method. If you disable basic authentication, keep in mind that this may prevent some clients from accessing mail remotely. Clients can log on only when you enable an authentication method that they support.

6. A default domain isn't set automatically. If you enable basic authentication, you can choose to set a default domain that should be used when no domain

Chapter 14

Managing Microsoft Outlook Web Access and HTTP Virtual Servers

In this chapter you'll learn how to manage Microsoft Outlook Web Access (OWA) and Hypertext Transfer Protocol (HTTP) virtual servers. Outlook Web Access is a standard Microsoft Exchange 2000 Server technology that allows users to access their mailboxes and public folder data using a Web browser. The technology works with standard Internet protocols, including Web Distributed Authoring and Versioning (WebDAV).

WebDAV is an extension to the HTTP that allows remote clients to create and manage server-based files, folders, and data. When users access mailboxes and public folders over the Web, an HTTP virtual server hosted by Exchange 2000 Server is working behind the scenes to grant access and transfer files to the browser. Because OWA doesn't need to be configured on the client, it's ideally suited for users who want to access e-mail while away from the office.

Mastering Outlook Web Access Essentials

When you install Exchange 2000 Server, OWA is automatically configured for use. This makes OWA fairly easy to manage, but there are some essential concepts that you should know in order to manage it more effectively. This section explains these concepts.

Using Outlook Web Access

OWA and a default HTTP virtual server are installed automatically when you install Exchange 2000 Server. In most cases you don't need to change any network options in order to allow users to access mailboxes and public folder data over the Web. You simply tell users the URL path that they need to type into their browser's Address field. The users can then access OWA when they're off-site.

OWA is designed to work with standard Web browsers, provided that the browsers support HTML 3.2 and JavaScript [European Computer Manufacturers Association (ECMA)] script. This means users could use Internet Explorer, Netscape Navigator, and other browsers to access OWA. However, Microsoft recommends that you use Internet Explorer 4.0 of later versions or Netscape Navigator 4.0+. Both browsers have been tested for compatibility with OWA.

Microsoft Internet Explorer version 5.0 and later have significant enhancements that make this browser a better choice for use with OWA. With Internet Explorer version 5.0 or later, you get performance that closely approximates Outlook 2000. Internet Explorer 5.0 presents a folder hierarchy that you can expand or collapse. Internet Explorer 5.0 supports drag-and-drop, HTML composition, and shortcut menus that you can access by right-clicking. The Application Programming Interface (API) for Internet Explorer 5.0 has extensions for OWA as well. These extensions allow Internet Explorer to perform functions locally instead of having to send requests to the server for processing. This reduces server load and improves performance. Other browsers and older versions of Internet Explorer don't support these advanced features.

OWA isn't a replacement for Outlook 2000, and although OWA supports many features of Outlook 2000, it doesn't support every feature. Specifically, OWA doesn't support

- Tasks, journals, and mailbox rules.
- Copying between public and private folders—but you can copy from one private folder to another.
- Voicemail and other telephony options.
- Offline access to e-mail.
- Spelling checker, calendar editing, and other advanced options.

You can configure OWA for single server and multiserver environments. In a single server environment, you use one server for all your messaging needs. Here, the HTTP virtual server used by OWA is configured directly on the Exchange server and you don't need to change any configuration options.

In a multiserver environment, you have separate servers for different messaging needs. Here, the HTTP virtual server used by OWA may reside on a different server than the servers used for Simple Mail Transfer Protocol (SMTP), Internet Message Access Protocol 4 (IMAP4), and Post Office Protocol 3 (POP3). To make the best use of OWA in a multiserver environment, you should designate an Exchange front-end server. The front-end server is the server to which users connect when they want to use OWA. You'll find more on front-end and back-end servers in the section of this chapter entitled "Configuring Front-End and Back-End Servers for Multiserver Organizations."

You can use OWA with firewalls. If your network has a firewall in front of the HTTP virtual server, you must open ports 80 and 443 to the Exchange server's IP address. By default, HTTP uses port 80 and Secure Sockets Layer (SSL) uses port 443.

You can also configure your network so that the HTTP virtual server is placed on an isolated network referred to as a Demilitarized Zone (DMZ). To do this, you need to install two firewalls: a DMZ firewall and an organizational firewall. You connect the DMZ firewall between the Internet and the front-end server. You connect the organizational firewall between the front-end server and the organization. In a two-firewall setup, you configure OWA by completing the following steps:

1. Install the DMZ firewall. Open ports 80 and 443 to the front-end server's IP address.

2. Install Exchange 2000 Server and then configure the server as a front-end server that will provide OWA services.

3. The front-end server will make connections to back-end servers and to the organization's *global catalog server*, which provides information needed for logon and directory searches. On the organizational firewall, open port 80 to the IP addresses for the back-end servers. Then open ports 389 and 3268 to the IP address for the global catalog server.

Note If SSL is enabled, and you want all Web browsers to use SSL exclusively, you don't need to open port 80 on the DMZ firewall. However, you still need to open port 80 on the organizational firewall.

Enabling and Disabling Web Access for Users

Exchange 2000 Server enables OWA for each user by default. If necessary, you can disable OWA for specific users. To do this, complete the following steps:

1. Start Active Directory Users And Computers.

2. From the View menu, select Advanced Features. Advanced features should now be enabled for viewing and configuring.

3. Double-click the user's name in Active Directory Users And Computers. This opens the Properties dialog box for the user account.

4. In the Exchange Advanced tab, click Protocol Settings, and then in the Protocols dialog box, double-click HTTP.

5. To disable Outlook Web Access for this user, clear Enable For Mailbox.

6. To enable Outlook Web Access for this user, select Enable For Mailbox.

7. Click OK three times.

Connecting to Mailboxes and Public Folders over the Web

You use WebDAV to access mailboxes and public folders over the World Wide Web and the corporate intranet. With WebDAV, clients can create and manage mailboxes and public folders directly in their browsers.

To access a public folder, type the folder's URL into Internet Explorer's Address field. For example, to access the public folder tree in a browser, type ***http://*** **servername/*public/***, where servername is a placeholder for the HTTP virtual server hosted by Exchange 2000 Server and *public* is the default name of the Public Folders Web share. You can access alternate public folder trees through their Web share as well. For example, you could access a public folder called Marketing on mailer1.domain.com using the following URL: *http://mailer1.domain.com/marketing/*. To access a mailbox, type the mailbox's URL into Internet Explorer's Address field. For example, to access the mailbox for the Exchange alias *williams*, type ***http://*servername/*Exchange/williams/***, where *servername* is a placeholder for the HTTP virtual server hosted by Exchange 2000 Server and *williams* is the alias of the Exchange mailbox you want to access.

 Note In both cases users need to authenticate themselves to be granted access. If users are unable to authenticate themselves, they see an error page and are denied access to Exchange data.

Managing HTTP Virtual Servers

This section examines key tasks that you use to manage HTTP virtual servers. HTTP virtual servers provide the transport services you need to access public folders and mailboxes from the Web. You can also use HTTP virtual servers to publish documents that can be accessed by off-site users or by the general public.

Creating Additional HTTP Virtual Servers

When you install Exchange 2000 Server, a default HTTP virtual server is installed and configured for use. The default HTTP virtual server allows authenticated users to access their mailboxes and public folder data. As your organization grows, you may find that you need additional HTTP virtual servers to handle the needs of remote users or that you want to offload HTTP services to separate Exchange servers. You can handle both of these tasks by installing Exchange 2000 Server on new servers and then creating additional HTTP virtual servers as necessary.

You can create additional HTTP virtual servers by completing the following steps:

1. If you're installing the virtual server on a new Exchange server, make sure that messaging services have been installed on the server.

2. If you want the HTTP virtual server to use a new IP address, you must configure the IP address before installing the HTTP virtual server. For details, refer to "Assigning a Static IP Address" in Chapter 15 of *Microsoft Windows 2000 Administrator's Pocket Consultant* (Microsoft Press, 2000).

3. Start System Manager. If administrative groups are enabled, expand the administrative group in which the server you want to use is located.

4. Navigate to the Protocols container in the console tree. Expand Servers, expand the server you want to work with, and then expand Protocols.

5. Right-click HTTP in the console tree, point to New, and then select HTTP Virtual Server. You should see the Properties dialog box shown in Figure 14-1.

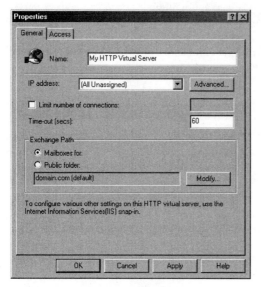

Figure 14-1. *Use the Properties dialog box to configure a new HTTP Virtual Server.*

6. In the Name field, type a descriptive name for the virtual server.

7. Use the IP Address selection list to select an available IP address. Choose (All Unassigned) to allow HTTP to respond on all unassigned IP addresses that are configured on the server. The TCP port is assigned automatically as port 80 for HTTP and port 443 for SSL.

8. To set additional identities, click Advanced in the General tab. Use the following options in the Advanced dialog box to modify the server's identity:

   - **Add**   Adds a new identity. Click Add, select the IP address you want to use, and then type a host name, TCP port, and SSL port. Click OK when you're finished.

   - **Modify**   Allows you to modify the currently selected entry in the Identities list box.

   - **Remove**   Allows you to remove the currently selected entry from the Identities list box.

Note The IP address/TCP port combination must be unique on every virtual server. Multiple virtual servers can use the same port, provided that the servers are configured to use different IP addresses.

9. Connection limits control the maximum number of simultaneous connections. To set a connection limit, select Limit Number Of Connections and then type a limit.

10. The Time-Out field controls the connection time-out. The default is 900 seconds. As necessary, type a new time-out value.

11. Click Finish to create the virtual server.

Configuring Ports, IP Addresses, and Host Names Used by HTTP Virtual Servers

Each HTTP virtual server is identified by a unique TCP port, SSL port, IP address, and host name. The default TCP port is 80. The default SSL port is 443. The default IP address setting is to use any available IP address. The default host name is the Exchange server's Domain Name System (DNS) name.

When the server is multihomed or when you use it to provide OWA/Web services for multiple domains, the default configuration isn't ideal. On a multihomed server, you'll usually want messaging protocols to respond on a specific IP address, and to do this, you need to change the default setting. On a server that provides OWA/Web services for multiple domains, you'll usually want to specify an additional host name for each domain.

To change the identity of an HTTP virtual server, complete the following steps:

1. If you're configuring a new Exchange server, ensure that messaging services have been installed on the server.

2. If you want the HTTP virtual server to use a new IP address, you must configure the IP address before trying to specify the IP address on the HTTP virtual server. For details, refer to "Assigning a Static IP Address" in Chapter 15 of *Microsoft Windows 2000 Administrator's Pocket Consultant.*

3. Start Internet Services Manager. Click Start, point to Programs, point to Administrative Tools, and select Internet Services Manager.

4. In the console tree, right-click Internet Information Services, and then select Connect.

5. In the Connect To Computer dialog box, type the name of the computer to which you want to connect, and then click OK.

6. In Internet Services Manager, each HTTP virtual server is represented by a Web site. The Default Web Site represents the default HTTP virtual server. Double-click the entry for the server you want to work with.

7. Right-click the Web site that you want to manage, and then select Properties.

8. In the Web Site tab, click Advanced. As Figure 14-2 shows, you can now use the Advanced Multiple Web Site Configuration dialog box to configure multiple identities for the virtual server.

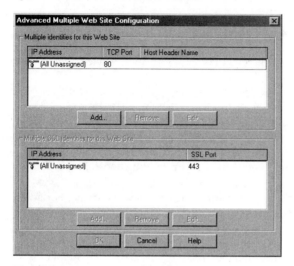

Figure 14-2. *You can use the Advanced Multiple Web Site Configuration dialog box to configure multiple identities for the virtual server.*

9. Use the Multiple Identities For This Web Site panel to manage TCP port settings:

- **Add** Adds a new identity. Click Add, select the IP address you want to use, and then type the TCP port and host name. Click OK when you're finished.

- **Edit** Allows you to edit the currently selected entry in the Identities list box.

- **Remove** Allows you to remove the currently selected entry from the Identities list box.

10. Use the Multiple SSL Identities For This Web Site panel to manage SSL port settings. Click Add to create new entries. Use Edit or Remove to modify or delete existing entries.

11. Click OK twice.

Enabling SSL on HTTP Virtual Servers

Secure Socket Layer (SSL) is a protocol for encrypting data that's transferred between a client and a server. Without SSL, servers pass data in clear text to clients, and this may be a security risk in an enterprise environment. With SSL, servers pass data encoded using 40-bit or 128-bit encryption.

While HTTP virtual servers are configured to use SSL on port 443 automatically, the server won't use SSL unless you've created and installed an X.509 certificate. You can create and install an X.509 certificate for an HTTP virtual server by completing the following steps:

1. Start Internet Services Manager. Click Start, point to Programs, point to Administrative Tools, and then select Internet Services Manager.

2. In the console tree, right-click Internet Information Services, and then select Connect.

3. In the Connect To Computer dialog box, type the name of the computer to which you want to connect, and then click OK.

4. In Internet Services Manager, each HTTP virtual server is represented by a Web site. The Default Web Site represents the default HTTP virtual server. Double-click the entry for the server you want to work with, and then right-click the Web site that you want to manage and choose Properties.

5. In the Directory Security tab, click Server Certificate. This starts the Web Server Certificate Wizard. Use the wizard to create a new certificate. For additional virtual servers on the same Exchange server, you'll want to assign an existing certificate.

6. Send the certificate request to your certificate authority (CA). When you receive the certificate back from the CA, access the Web Server Certificate Wizard from the virtual server's Properties dialog box again. Now you'll be able to process the pending request and install the certificate.

Restricting Incoming Connections and Setting Time-Out Values

You control incoming connections to an HTTP virtual server in two ways. You can set a limit on the number of simultaneous connections, and you can set a connection time-out value.

Normally, virtual servers accept an unlimited number of connections, and this is an optimal setting in most environments. However, when you're trying to prevent a virtual server from becoming overloaded, you may want to limit the number of simultaneous connections. Once the limit is reached, no other clients are permitted to access the server. The clients must wait until the connection load on the server decreases.

The connection time-out value determines when idle user sessions are disconnected. With the default HTTP virtual server, sessions time out after they've been idle for 900 seconds (15 minutes). While 15 minutes may seem short, it's a sound security policy to disconnect idle sessions and force users to log back on to the server. If you don't disconnect idle sessions within a reasonable amount of time, unauthorized persons may gain access to your messaging system through a browser window left unattended on a remote terminal.

Using SMTP Queues

Each SMTP virtual server has several system queues associated with it. These queues are

- **Local Delivery** Contains messages that are queued for local delivery—that is, messages that the Exchange server is waiting to deliver to a local Exchange mailbox.

- **Messages Awaiting Directory Lookup** Contains messages to recipients who have not yet been resolved in Active Directory.

- **Messages Waiting To Be Routed** Contains messages waiting to be routed to a destination server. Messages move from here to a link queue.

- **Final Destination Currently Unreachable** Contains messages that can't be routed because the destination server is unreachable.

- **Pre-Submission** Contains messages that have been acknowledged and accepted by the SMTP service but haven't been processed yet.

As you can see, SMTP queues are used to hold messages in various stages of routing. You access these queues through the SMTP virtual server node by completing the following steps:

1. Start System Manager. If administrative groups are enabled, expand the administrative group in which the server you want to use is located.

2. Navigate to the Protocols container in the console tree. Expand Servers, expand the server you want to work with, and then expand Protocols.

3. Navigate to a virtual server's Queues node. Expand SMTP, expand the virtual server you want to work with, and then expand Queues.

4. Select the queue you want to work with.

Using Microsoft MTA (X.400) Queues

The Microsoft Message Transfer Agent (MTA) provides addressing and routing information for sending messages from one server to another. The MTA relies on X.400 transfer stacks to provide additional details for message transfer, and these stacks are similar in purpose to the Exchange virtual servers used with SMTP.

The key queue used with the Microsoft MTA is the PendingRerouteQ. This queue contains messages that are waiting to be rerouted after a temporary link outage. To access the PendingRerouteQ, follow these steps:

1. Start System Manager. If administrative groups are enabled, expand the administrative group in which the server you want to use is located.

2. Navigate to the Protocols container in the console tree. Expand Servers, expand the server you want to work with, and then expand Protocols.

3. Expand X.400, and then expand Queues. Finally, select PendingRerouteQ.

Using MAPI Queues

Novell GroupWise, Lotus Notes, and Lotus cc:Mail connectors all use MAPI queues. MAPI queues are used to route and deliver messages over the related connector. The queues you may see are

- **MTS-In** Contains messages that have come to the Exchange organization over the connector. The message contents and addresses haven't been converted to Exchange format.

- **Ready-In** Contains messages that have been converted to Exchange format and are ready to be delivered. Recipient addresses still need to be resolved.

- **Ready-Out** Contains messages that have been prepared for delivery to a foreign system. The message addresses have been resolved, but the message contents haven't been converted.

- **Badmail** Contains all messages that caused errors when the connector tried to process them. No further delivery attempts are made on these messages and they are stored in this queue until you delete them manually.

To access a MAPI queue, follow these steps:

1. Start System Manager. If administrative groups are enabled, expand the administrative group you want to work with.

2. If available, expand Routing Groups , and then expand the routing group that contains the connector you want to work with.

3. Navigate to the connector's Queues node. Expand Connectors, expand the connector, and then expand Queues.

4. Select the queue you want to work with.

Managing Queues

You usually won't see messages in queues because they're processed and routed quickly. Messages come into a queue, Exchange Server performs a lookup or establishes a connection, and then Exchange Server either moves the message to a new queue or delivers it to its destination.

Messages remain in a queue when there's a problem. To check for problem messages, you must enumerate messages in the queue. Messages aren't enumerated by default—you must do this manually.

Enumerating Messages in Queues

In order to manage queues, you must enumerate messages. This process allows you to examine queue contents and perform management tasks on messages within a particular queue.

The easiest way to enumerate messages is to do so in sets of 100. To display the first 100 messages in a queue, follow these steps:

1. Start System Manager, and then navigate to the queue you want to work with.

2. Right-click the queue, and then select Enumerate 100 Messages.

Repeat this process if you want to access the next 100 messages. Or to refresh the current list of messages, right-click the queue, and then select Re-enumerate.

Note   You can only re-enumerate a queue that you've managed previously. If you haven't enumerated a queue previously, the Details pane will display the following message: Enumerate messages from the queue node. Additionally, if there are no messages in the queue, the Details pane will display the following message: There are no matching messages queued.

You can also use a custom filter to enumerate messages. To create a custom filter and then set the filter as the default, follow these steps:

1. Start System Manager, and then navigate to the queue you want to work with.

2. Right-click the queue, and then select Custom Filter.

3. From the Action selection list, select Enumerate.

4. To select a specific number of messages, choose Select Only The, and then specify the Number Of Messages to enumerate.

5. To select messages by other criteria, choose Select Messages That Are, and then set the enumeration criteria.

6. To select all available messages, choose Select All Messages.

7. Optionally, you can save your changes as the default filter by selecting Set As Default Filter.

8. When you click OK, the custom filter is automatically executed.

Understanding Queue Summaries and Queue States

Whenever you click a Queues node in System Manager, you get a summary of the currently available queues for the selected node. These queues can include both system and link queues, depending on the state of the Exchange server.

Although queue summaries provide important details for troubleshooting message flow problems, you do have to know what to look for. The connection state is the key information to look at first. This value tells you the state of the queue. States you'll see include

- **Active**   An active queue is needed to allow messages to be transported out of a link queue.

- **Ready**   A ready queue is needed to allow messages to be transported out of a system queue. When link queues are ready, they can have a connection allocated to them.

- **Retry**   A connection attempt has failed and the server is waiting to retry.

- **Scheduled**   The server is waiting for a scheduled connection time.

- **Remote**   The server is waiting for a remote dequeue command (TURN/ ETRN).

- **Frozen**   The queue is frozen, and none of its messages can be processed for routing. Messages can enter the queue, however, as long as the Exchange routing categorizer is running. You must unfreeze the queue to resume normal queue operations.

Administrators can choose to enable or disable connections to queues. If connections are disabled, the queue is unable to route and deliver messages.

You can change the queue state to Active by using the FORCE CONNECTION command. When you do this, Exchange Server should immediately enable a connection for the queue, which will allow messages to be routed and delivered from it. You can force a connection to change the Retry or Scheduled state as well.

Other summary information that you may find useful in troubleshooting includes:

- **Time Of Submission Of Oldest Msg**   Tells you when the oldest message was sent by a client. Any time the oldest message has been in the queue for several days, you have a problem with message delivery. Either Exchange Server is having a problem routing that specific message, or a deeper routing problem may be affecting the organization.

- **Total # Of Msgs**   Tells you the total number of messages waiting in the queue. If you see a large number of messages waiting in the queue, you may have a connectivity or routing problem.

- **Total Msg Size (KB)**   Tells you the total size of all messages in the queue. Large messages can take a long time to deliver, and, as a result, they may slow down message delivery.

- **Time Of Next Connection Retry**   When the connection state is Retry, this column tells you when another connection attempt will be made. You can use Force Connection to attempt a connection immediately.

Viewing Message Details

Anytime a message is displayed in a queue, you can double-click it to view message details. The details provide additional information that identifies the message, including a message ID that you can use with message tracking.

Enabling and Disabling Connections to Queues

The only way to enable and disable connections to queues is on a global basis, which means that you enable or disable all queues for a given SMTP virtual server,

MTA object, or connector. Enabling queues makes the queues available for routing and delivery. Disabling queues makes the queues unavailable for routing and delivery.

To enable or disable connections to queues, follow these steps:

1. Start System Manager.

2. Navigate to the Queues node for the SMTP virtual server, MTA object, or connector you want to manage.

3. To enable connections to all queues, right-click the Queues node, and then select Enable All Connections.

4. To disable connections to all queues, right-click the Queues node, and then select Disable All Connections.

Forcing Connections to Queues

In most cases you can change the queue state to Active by forcing a connection. Simply right-click the queue, and then select Force Connection. When you do this, Exchange Server should immediately enable connections to the queue, and this should allow messages to be routed and delivered from it.

Freezing and Unfreezing Queues

When you freeze a queue, all message transfer out of that queue stops. This means that messages can continue to enter the queue but no messages will leave it. To restore normal operations, you must unfreeze the queue.

You freeze and then unfreeze a queue by completing the following steps:

1. Start System Manager, and then navigate to the queue you want to work with.

2. Enumerate the queue so that you can see the messages it contains.

3. Right-click the queue, and then select Freeze All Messages.

4. When you're done troubleshooting, right-click the queue, and then select Unfreeze All Messages.

Another way to freeze messages in a queue is to do so selectively. In this way, you can control the transport of a single message or several messages that may be causing problems on the server. For example, if a large message is delaying the delivery of other messages, you can freeze the message until other messages have left the queue. Afterward, you can unfreeze the message to resume normal delivery.

To freeze and then unfreeze an individual message, complete the following steps:

1. Start System Manager, and then navigate to the queue you want to work with.

2. Enumerate messages in the queue.

3. Right-click the problem message, and then select Freeze.

4. When you're ready to resume delivery of the message, right-click the problem message, and then select Unfreeze.

Deleting Messages from Queues

You can remove messages from queues in several ways. To delete all messages in a queue, follow these steps:

1. Start System Manager, and then navigate to the queue you want to work with.
2. Enumerate the messages in the queue to make sure that you really want to delete all the messages that the queue contains.
3. Right-click the queue, and then select one of the following options:

    - **Delete All Messages (No NDR)**   Deletes all messages from the queue without sending a nondelivery report to the sender
    - **Delete All Messages (Send NDR)**   Deletes all messages from the queue and notifies the sender with a nondelivery report

4. When prompted, click Yes to confirm the deletion.

To delete messages selectively, follow these steps:

1. Start System Manager, and then navigate to the queue you want to work with.
2. Enumerate messages in the queue.
3. Right-click the message or messages that you want to delete, and then select one of the following options:

    - **Delete Messages (No NDR)**   Deletes the selected messages from the queue without sending a nondelivery report to the sender.
    - **Delete Messages (Send NDR)**   Deletes the selected messages from the queue and notifies the sender with a nondelivery report.

4. When prompted, click Yes to confirm the deletion.

Deleting messages from a queue removes them from the messaging system permanently. You can't recover the deleted messages.

Index

Note to reader Italics are used to indicate references to illustrations.